The Empath and the Dark Road

REDFeather™

MIND | BODY | SPIRIT

An Imprint of Schiffer Publishing, Ltd.

The Empath and the Dark Road

STRUGGLES THAT TEACH THE GIFT

Bety Comerford & Steve Wilson

Other Schiffer Books by the Authors:

The Reluctant Empath
ISBN: 978-0-7643-4603-3

The Empath's Quest: Finding Your Destiny
ISBN: 978-0-7643-5223-2

The Empathic Ghost Hunter
ISBN: 978-0-7643-5409-0

The Empathic Oracle (with Michelle Motuzas Johnson)
ISBN: 978-0-7643-5590-5

Designed by Justin Watkinson

Type set in NewBskvll BT/Minion Pro

ISBN: 978-0-7643-5591-2
Printed in China

Published by Schiffer Publishing, Ltd.
4880 Lower Valley Road
Atglen, PA 19310
Phone: (610) 593-1777; Fax: (610) 593-2002
E-mail: Info@schifferbooks.com
Web: www.schifferbooks.com

For our complete selection of fine books on this and related subjects, please visit our website at www.schifferbooks.com. You may also write for a free catalog.

Schiffer Publishing's titles are available at special discounts for bulk purchases for sales promotions or premiums. Special editions, including personalized covers, corporate imprints, and excerpts, can be created in large quantities for special needs. For more information, contact the publisher.

We are always looking for people to write books on new and related subjects.
If you have an idea for a book, please contact us at proposals@schifferbooks.com.

FROM BETY: To all of you who take a chance, pick up our books, and approach our words with an open heart and an open mind. We write these for you.

FROM STEVE: To those who have crossed my path, both student and teacher, who have taught me that the best teacher is the one who continues to be the student.

Contents

Introduction

Is it possible there are unseen things that feed off the darker aspects of human emotion? Do they have the ability to manipulate us? Do we manipulate ourselves with our own dark thoughts? Do we manipulate each other from some unknown place within us that stems from a place of lack and fear? Does this place of lack and fear make us feel threatened? Not worthy to touch the truth that is always around us?

How many times have we wondered why bad things happen to good people? How often have the mystics and religious figures tried to explain why this occurs? Some call it karma. Some call it bad luck. We believe it's all part of the life that teaches the empath—a sort of energetic boot camp that leads you to learn and understand the power of who you truly are. It all culminates in the knowing that you are part of the same collective consciousness. We all feel, and we all experience each other throughout our days, throughout our lives, trying to understand, or trying to avoid, that which is uncomfortable— what some call the dark moments of life. Good, bad, or indifferent, we as empaths know we can't escape the experiences of how we and others feel.

The world is so caught up in pointing out differences between us that we forget we are the same, sitting in darkness, craving the light.

Many spiritual teachers strive to keep their students ignorant of the darker aspects of spirituality. They reason that it does no good to scare their students . . . or believe none are capable of navigating this dark road. However, try as we may, the dark road, with its many twists and turns, is only a heartbeat away. We have always felt that this is a disservice to the persons who seek to understand their spiritual paths, especially those whose path includes the gift of empathy.

There is a balance to everything. Without dark, there can be no light. In fact, we believe darkness is simply an absence of light. The people who challenge you and hurt you in life add to your understanding of the teachings of cause and effect. Even though you may not realize it during your challenging times when your emotions begin to overwhelm, there are always options on how you respond. Do you respond with anger, victimhood, envy, or jealousy—all negative emotions that create a heaviness and drain on your own energy? When you react in anger, victimhood, or other lesser energies, they become your story, seemingly etched in stone that now controls your life.

Is it possible you can respond in the knowing that there is always a higher experience that can be drawn on that begins to give you freedom from emotional drama?

We say yes.

It's the beginning of an understanding of what an empath is really experiencing—the energy of choice. You can choose to surround yourself in a container that is filled with bitter vinegar. Or you can surround yourself in a container that is filled with sweet, honeyed wine. Herein lies the learning and the choices presented to you by those who challenge you as you walk your path. It isn't always pretty or well landscaped, but it provides such an opportunity to attain a more balanced, fulfilled life.

What about those dark shadows that go bump in the night? The ones that haunt the dreamtime? The ones that stalk you as you go about your daily life? Do they torment you? Do they amplify your own personal torments? Believe it or not, even they serve a purpose. Without them, you would never learn your own courage and strength as you release yourself from being the wounded prey they seek. Fear is the blood they smell on the wind. Courage is the armor that keeps them at bay.

We decided to write this book because there is another way of living your life. Of not constantly reacting to fear and misunderstanding. It's important that you, as an empath, who is already so sensitive to energy, learn and understand why dark figures appear after you turn off the lights. Why your hair stands on end for no reason. Why you seem to attract challenging people into your sphere. So many of our students have come to us with these issues. As we say, you must be doing something right if something cares enough to bother you.

As an empath, you will already have learned that you can't hide away from these challenges forever. If you truly wish to stand in your power and take your place in the world, you will need to confront and understand the dark underbelly of your path. Once you do, these challenges many times disappear because they are no longer teaching you what it is you're here to learn—the power of your energy.

It isn't easy. We'll be the first to admit that. However, the alternative is a life half lived, a life full of fear and anger and frustration. A life that indeed becomes a banquet for the darker aspects of emotion to feed off. A life in which you stand front and center as a victim.

There is no condemnation here. It is simply part of the learning curve of what it means to be human, and of how energetically powerful you really are once you learn to get out of your own way.

As we have done in our previous books on empathy, in order to make the subject easier to comprehend, we are using Alex as our stand-in. Everything we have written here has actually happened to us.

If we can survive, so can you.

Outside In

1

It was Saturday afternoon. Alex watched his students file in and take their seats. He'd begun teaching classes in spirituality several years earlier; he always felt gratified when he was able to help people make sense of things they once considered nonsensical. It helped him realize, once again, how right he'd been to share his experiences with others.

Today he was teaching one of his favorite subjects: what it means to be empathic. He'd lost count of how many individuals entered his classes over the years, all of whom were convinced there was something wrong with them. Why were they feeling as much as they were? The question most often asked was "How do I turn all this off and get back to what is normal?" However, what exactly is "normal"? What's normal for one person may not be normal for another. Then there were those skeptics who doubted they even had a gift in the first place.

He looked at the faces of his newest batch of students and immediately recognized those who couldn't yet admit they were empathic, but were curious nevertheless. He saw those who wanted to understand their empathic abilities and those who couldn't wait to dive in to discover what it all meant and whether it could be fixed.

"Good afternoon, everyone. Thank you all for having the courage to come here today. I promise I won't bite." There were a few twitters in the room. "My name is Alex, and I'm going to teach you what a wondrous gift empathy truly is."

Some students rolled their eyes in doubt, while others leaned ever so slightly forward in their chairs, ready to listen. To learn. To understand.

After sharing a bit about his own background and how he'd come to this point in his life, Alex then went around the room and asked the students to do the same. He sensed there were those who wouldn't share, while there were others who couldn't wait to share what they thought was *wrong* with them.

The first to speak was a red-haired woman in her early thirties. She gave an embarrassed smile as she introduced herself. "Hi, I'm Judy. I'm here tonight because I've spent my entire life breaking down into sobs if someone looks at me funny. Or if I see traumatic events on TV and magazines. And don't even get me started on sad, sappy movies."

Alex smiled. "I'd say you're sensitive to emotional cues. Whenever one of those occurs, you instantly react to them. I'm sure I can show you some skills to help you live your life in a more balanced way."

An older gentleman next spoke. "My name is William. I'll be honest. I'm not sure about this stuff, but I know that when I get into a crowd, all I can think about is getting the hell out of there and finding the nearest closet to hide in."

Several laughed in agreement.

As more students shared, Alex sensed them beginning to feel safe, especially when they realized they were not alone in what they'd been going through.

"I have one for you!" a swarthy young man spoke up. "What about feeling angry? Or sad for no apparent reason? It's not fair. I feel like I'm living on a roller coaster of other people's emotions. I can't climb out of it. My chest hurts; my head aches. I feel like I want to throw up. I don't even want to leave my house anymore. What's that all about?"

Everyone raised their hands, chiming in with their own stories. The room filled with the energy of the people in the group needing to share their emotional truth.

There was only one person who wasn't engaged in what was happening. It was a young woman who sat in the back of the room. She watched the others, a wall of silent resistance encasing her. As Alex gauged the energy of the students, his attention continually strayed to her. Their eyes met. There was something about her. It had nothing to do with her dark attractive looks or the classic black outfit she wore. It had to do with the harried look in her brown eyes and with her general demeanor. If he had to put a word to what he was seeing, he'd have to say she looked haunted. Not so much by a ghost, but by a worrying fear that was eating her up alive.

A few moments later, he saw how right he was. Determined to get her to engage, he pointed to her.

"Why are you here tonight?" he asked.

He watched as several emotions raced over her features, the most prominent being that of fear. But fear of what? Fear of ridicule? Fear of exposing a deep-seated dread? Or was it a fear of something so insidious, she was too terrified to put it into words? He had no choice but to wait, hoping she'd answer his question. Finally, she sighed.

"I'm not sure how to answer that," she admitted.

"Believe me, there isn't anything I haven't heard or been through myself when it comes to being an empath."

She hesitated, not sure whether to believe him or not. However, realizing that if she didn't speak, she'd miss the opportunity to have her concerns addressed, she took a deep breath and let it out slowly.

"What are these cold, black things I see and feel? They keep trying to get close to me, especially at night when I'm trying to sleep. And when I finally do fall asleep, they invade my dreams. I've been to counseling. All they do is tell me it's all in my head. That what I'm experiencing isn't real. I've been to the doctors to see if maybe there's something physically wrong with me, but despite running all sorts of tests, they find nothing. Frankly, I'm desperate for answers. What is this? How do I make them go away?"

Alex felt the energy abruptly shift. The eagerness to share quickly turned to an icy chill, as if someone had flipped a switch. As if this woman was the only one to dare speak of these darker entities they'd all experienced, but lacked the courage to acknowledge. The room immediately fell silent, all eyes focused expectantly on Alex, waiting to see if he had the answer to make their emotional ups and downs magically go away.

He was suddenly thrust back to another time and place, to the years when he'd been a teenager, struggling to understand who he was and why he felt all that he did. When he too was besieged by the cold, dark beings the young woman had described. Before he could stop it, memories flooded in. Time stood still, and the classroom faded away as the reminiscences took hold.

Alex grew up in a small town in Massachusetts. From the time he was first conscious of the world around him, he knew he was different. Unlike his brothers and sisters, he seemed to feel things deeper—more acutely. He knew when people lied. He knew when they were sad or angry or depressed, without them having to say a word. He didn't know how he knew all these things, but he did. Many times these physical sensations manifested themselves as a pain in his stomach or in his heart. Or as an overpowering anxiety—as if he wanted to jump out of his skin. It was so draining; he disliked being around other people. But of course that didn't always work. In those situations where he had to be around others, he tried his best to keep things light and positive. It was the only way for him to survive his life, or so he thought.

High school proved to be challenging. He felt out of sorts and uncoordinated in his own body. Looking around him at the various cliques, he definitely didn't fit into what his fellow students believed was important. He wasn't into sports and definitely wasn't into the science or literary clubs. Despite that, he really wanted to belong somewhere. Anywhere. Unfortunately, he came off to his fellow students as a loner. Not because he was, but because he didn't know how else to be. Overwhelmed by all their emotions, he kept to himself, adding to the aura of being a lone wolf.

As he went from class to class in his daily routine, he noticed how constricted he felt in his own body. While listening to the teacher drone on, he experienced random thoughts that seemed to come out of nowhere. They were dark in nature—challenging him to get up and walk out of class. Or to simply quit and never return to school. The more disturbing thoughts popped in when he was driving. What if he were to turn the steering wheel ever so slightly and aim his car into oncoming traffic?

These thoughts frightened him. Where were they coming from? Were they even his thoughts? Did they belong to someone else? Why was this happening to him? Overhearing his parents, he sometimes heard stories about relatives who were considered crazy, strange, eccentric. Whenever he brought this up to his mother, she'd shush him, as if these family members needed to remain a buried secret.

Had he inherited the crazy genes? Was he going to become one of *those* relatives whom everyone spoke about in whispers? Was he already?

He found himself obsessing about these thoughts. The more he obsessed, the more he felt anxious. And jumpy. His only solace was nature and playing guitar, and he held onto those for dear life. He clung to the few friends he had, but even there, he sensed a growing distance. They weren't feeling what he was feeling. They didn't understand what he was going through. There were times he was convinced he was only one step ahead of these dark thoughts, never daring to look back unless they catch up and devour him. The result of this worry was a growing debilitating heaviness in his own body that refused to go away.

Could these thoughts be a result of his inability to fit in at school? Or worse. Was he going crazy?

In order to combat these distressing notions, he made a point of trying to be whatever his classmates thought he should be. They all seemed normal. None of them spoke of having crazy thoughts or relatives who might be certifiable. Since they knew what it was like to be normal, he tried his best to emulate them. Yet, no matter how hard he tried, the aura of loner still clung to him.

He knew he wasn't helping himself by making the conscious decision to dress differently or wear his hair a little longer than everyone else did. Despite his desperation to belong, there was still a part of his psyche that clung to discovering his own identity. Of really wanting to know who he truly was. The clothes and the long hair were part of this quest.

It was a two-edged sword. He wanted to fit in, yet he needed to have an identity of his own. He didn't want to be the outcast, or stand out, but part of him rebelled against being exactly like everyone else. Of having a cookie-cutter personality. No matter how he tried to convince himself otherwise, the truth was that it just didn't feel right to dress and act exactly like the other students.

Although he was too young to understand it at the time, this would turn into a very big lesson in his life.

It was near the Thanksgiving break when Alex made his way down the corridor toward his English literature class. He had his mind on the quiz he was about to take on the work of Ernest Hemingway. Just as he rounded the corner, he noticed a trio of football players walking toward him. They hadn't noticed him yet in the crowd of teenagers running toward their respective classes, but there was something about them that immediately put Alex on his guard. He knew who they were; he'd watched their games. They'd even nodded to him in passing on other days. However, on that particular morning, for whatever reason, his instincts were on full alert—a foreboding that something unpleasant was about to happen.

Maybe if I keep my head down, I'll get past them, and they won't even see me.

Unfortunately, he raised his eyes to take one last look to make sure he didn't crash into them. And caught the eye of the biggest player.

"Hey, freak!" His heart sank, and before he could stop himself, his limbs began to shake. "What's with the long hair, freak? You think you're some kind of rock star or something?"

Surrounded by mocking laughter from the other students, Alex knew it would be suicidal to respond. Instead, he fell back upon a technique he'd learned growing up whenever his father screamed at him. He felt himself crawling into a familiar black space in an effort to disappear. Covering himself up with a cocoon, it was as though he had the ability to leave his body and not hear what was being said to him. Out of sight, out of mind—like it used to be during the confrontations with his father.

The problem was, he couldn't completely tune everyone out. This learned ability from childhood was failing him now. He was conscious of every eye in the hallway staring at him. In the midst of the staring, he felt the thoughts of many—*thank God it's not me they're picking on.* It set him apart even more. His energetic self-esteem—that is, the ability to discern where his own energy began and ended—pooled out of him as the players threw his books to the floor, their scornful laughter echoing down the hallway.

All the skills he'd used to keep himself apart from others, not to be a target, to hold some kind of personal space, failed. He felt himself filling up with the thoughts and emotional energy of the surrounding students. In the past, this focus had allowed him to get through difficult situations. But now, it was too much. He felt exposed. And vulnerable.

As the players continued to rain verbal abuse upon him, he crawled further into himself, trying to search for anything that could shield him from their vicious taunts. Unfortunately, he didn't realize that as he pulled away from them, their words, energy, and emotions were withdrawing with him, stuck like barbs in his own energy. Instead of feeling safe, he now felt imprisoned in a hole of despair.

He was literally saved by the bell when it clanged, sending the players and students scurrying to their classrooms. Alone now, Alex slowly pulled himself out from his self-imposed cocoon. As he picked up his books from the floor, he felt heavy, disoriented. Completely drained. As if he'd been turned inside out both emotionally and physically. The cruelest emotion he felt, though, was a self-loathing that wouldn't let go. He'd done nothing to defend himself. He'd stood there like a weakling and allowed them to humiliate him. In reality, there was nothing he could have done. If he'd tried to defend himself, they would have beaten him to a pulp. Nevertheless, he felt the reverberations of their disdain. Worse, he felt the disdain of the other students. In their eyes, he was nothing but a coward. A fool. A nothing.

Still shaking, his emotions in a turmoil, it was impossible to go to class. Instead, he turned and walked out the front door, down the steps and into a copse of woods that lay near the parking lot of the high school. He headed toward the tallest oak and sat with his back up against the trunk. Burying his face in his arms, he tried to forget about the experience. Tried to move beyond their words and malicious taunts. But he couldn't. It was as if they'd taken a magic marker and written the unbearable expressions all over his skin: *weirdo, freak, loser, coward.*

They weren't true. He tried to tell himself they weren't true. But in that moment, he believed they were. He sat under the oak for an hour, working through what he was feeling. As he finally reached a space where he could step back from the pain and humiliation, he felt his feet tingle. Ever so slowly, the debilitating energies began to seep out of him. As they did so, he could see clearer, think clearer. Comprehend better without his mind muddled with all that heavier, draining energy.

The jocks, not only those who had picked on him, but the others on the sports teams, all looked alike. They dressed alike, used the same expressions, and even had nicknames for each other. It occurred to Alex that the reason they did this was to set themselves apart from the others. To show they were superior to everyone else. To validate their specialness. And in that need to validate their specialness, they *took* energy from others. They'd certainly taken his today.

It was the same with the prettiest girls in school. They too dressed alike, spoke their own special language, and made sure to keep themselves disdainfully apart from all the other girls. They did this in order to announce their specialness to the rest of the school.

None of these cliques had ever felt good to Alex. They made his stomach clench whenever he was near them. Although he didn't yet understand that he was an empath, he knew enough to realize that although they took others' energy, he definitely didn't want or need their energy.

Wait a minute. Is it possible those guys took my energy because I allowed it to happen? By reacting the way I did, was I responsible for making it easy for them to take my energy? Is that why I felt so exhausted and out of sorts?

As the realization hit him, he felt a lighter, calming sensation flow through him. It was an energy with no judgment. No agenda. It had no need to humiliate. The heaviness in his heart slowly flowed out of him until he no longer felt inside out. Where was this energy coming from? Who was it coming from?

He knew something was happening that he needed to understand. What he was feeling in that moment wasn't occurring by accident. It was trying to teach him. But what was the lesson?

The Difference between Being **Sensitive** and Being **Empathic**

We all have emotional moments in our lives—triggers that bring us back to a place of anger, sadness, or happiness. All these emotional moments are learned lessons from things in your past. It's as if some part of you has deemed that this is a good thing or a bad thing, and you respond accordingly. When something comes along that doesn't fit into what you believe "good" is, you have an emotional response.

As an empath, you experience these emotional moments a bit differently. You actually take on the energy of the projection of another's emotion or judgment. This is especially true when you are "picked out of the herd" by someone else's strong judgment, strong condemnation, or strong dislike of you that had no rhyme or reason to it. It is as if you are a sponge of every emotion and thought that surrounds you.

Part of the dark road of an empath is the unfortunate fact that you get picked out of the herd more than most people because you are a bit out of step with everyone else. You find yourself living a different lifestyle because of your sensitivity. You isolate yourself, attempt to stay in the shadows, and try hard not to call attention to yourself, yet, at the same time, you are dressing or acting differently because, like Alex, you are desperate to find your own identity. Why? Because you need to feel where you begin. Where you are not being the chameleon, trying to fit into others' conception of who you think they need you to be. Or who you think you need to be to fit in.

Many empaths are bullied because they are different. Yet, at some point, you begin to realize that those who bully and attack are only trying to hold power over you because of their own insecurities. Eventually you learn that power doesn't come from another human being. It comes from a higher source. Yet, until that lesson is learned, you remain the chameleon, trying desperately to fit in, to belong, forgetting or ignoring who you are learning to be in the process.

It is important, however, to understand what the difference is between being empathic and being sensitive. These qualities *are* different. A sensitive person is one who feels compassion for another. One who may feel sorry for others or commiserate with what they're going through, because perhaps they've gone through the same thing. The emotional cues from their past trigger the same emotional response in the present.

An empath may also do this, but it goes deeper. An empath is someone who *physically* feels what others are going through. If they are sad, you physically feel their sadness. If they're in pain, you physically feel their pain. Their emotions and reactions to their environment release an energy that you, as an empath, soak up. Negative emotional reactions from others equal negative physical and emotional reactions for the empath. Sensitives are dealing only with their own reactions, while empaths are dealing with a double-edged sword—feeling their own reaction along with the reaction of the other person. Is it possible that we can change our own reaction, thereby changing the experience of what we feel from others?

The Chameleon

The bullying continued. Alex took different corridors and timed his comings and goings to avoid running into the jocks.

There had to be a better way, another way to exist without always hiding. He grew tired of trying to figure out why he was being singled out.

Maybe part of the reason was the fact that he was such a loner. If he made an effort to reach out and make more friends, would the bullying stop?

He had no choice but to try. The alternative was to continue to live a furtive life, like a mouse constantly on the run. Or a prey animal trying its best to avoid predators.

Alex set out to strike up conversations with people who caught his eye, people who didn't make his stomach clench in fear or apprehension. Little by little, he began to cultivate a small group of friends with shared commonalities, the biggest of which was music. They all loved grunge rock, and they spent hours dissecting the lyrics of bands such as Nirvana and Pearl Jam. The music gave them a voice. For the first time, Alex felt like he finally belonged.

With this new group of friends, he grew confident. With his newfound confidence came an easing of the bullying, as if they recognized that he was no longer the freakish loner who didn't belong anywhere. It was harder to attack a group than one person. There was comfort in numbers.

It wouldn't be until later in his life that Alex would realize that on an unconscious level, the jocks felt fear—his fear—and reacted on it. The energy of fear released an energetic current that flowed out of him each time his fear was triggered. Once his confidence grew, the fear dissolved. The energetic current was broken. Without the fear to act on, he was no longer a viable target for the bullies to take advantage of.

But, as with most things in Alex's life, there was a lesson to be learned. And the lesson had to do with what he later came to call "chameleon-ing." Chameleons are lizards that have evolved a unique defense mechanism. In order to avoid predators, they change their physical colors to blend in. Alex found himself doing the same thing on an energetic level.

As his small circle of friends grew, there were two who stood out. They spent their time complaining about everything—about life, about themselves, about the fact that nothing was ever going to change. Before he could stop, Alex found himself listening and agreeing with everything they said. He felt caught up in their energy. They were right. Life was tough. People were tough. All this talk about love and peace was a crock. The three validated each other's feelings and emotions. For the first time, Alex didn't feel alone in feeling like a freak or a loser. These guys felt the same desolation he did.

Yet, every time he walked away from their bitch fest, the good feeling disappeared, leaving him drained and uneasy. His emotions began to boomerang. When he was together with these friends and they complained about the world, he felt great. When he walked away, he'd drop into the depths of despair.

What the hell was going on?

Once again he took himself into the woods, where he felt the most comfortable. Trying to figure all this out, it slowly dawned on him that, away from them, he really didn't think the world was so hopeless. Nor did he honestly believe that he was such a loser. Yet, when he was with the doomsday duo, as he'd started to call them, he realized he was allowing himself to get sucked into their drama in order to placate them. To once again feel as though he was part of a group.

When I do that, though, I'm not being authentic to myself. And I know I'm not because every time I leave them, I feel heavy and crummy, as though their words are glued onto me, and I can't get rid of them.

Each time he was with the doomsday duo, he was chameleon-ing. They were a little motley crew of losers who kept validating each other's sense of being losers. Did he really want that kind of energy? Did he really want to continue to feel awful every time he unplugged from them and walked away?

Jeez, I'm basically going down their rabbit hole of doom and gloom just to feel like I belong.

Yes, he'd felt marginalized in his life. He was beginning to understand that as an empath, he was like a giant Velcro wall where the thoughts, projections, releases, and emotions of everyone around him were stuck to him. The only way these balls of goo were going to fall off his Velcro wall was when he allowed them to fall off. When he stopped taking them on as his, as he was doing with the doomsday duo.

I don't need to keep reinventing myself every time I'm with a different group of people. Each time I do that, I sink into the energetic swamp they've created.

At the same time, Alex didn't want to lose that sense of belonging. Of being with a group of people who liked him. Somewhere within was the authentic Alex, even though he wasn't quite sure who that was yet. Nor did he know how to maneuver these interpersonal relationships without losing himself in them. He knew he didn't want to get slimed either with their energy or his own.

There had to be more to this. There had to be a better way of existing. He hoped that the answer would present itself quickly.

Being **Authentic**

As you know, until you learn the different flavors of what being an energetic human being is all about, you will continue to reinvent yourself. You will lose yourself in your marginalized feelings, forgetting those moments when you've felt the higher vibrations, whether walking in the woods, sitting by the ocean, or doing something else you love.

How many times have you tried your best to fit in with one person, two people, or a group, only to feel afterward as though you've been slimed? You've taken on their opinions, their thoughts, and their emotions in order to feel as though you belong. What if the next time the situation comes up, you instead make the conscious decision to simply be present to the experience. Not to hear and see what is going on around you, but to feel it. This is part of learning who you are. The outside (that part of us we endeavor to be to others) shows you who you are not. Each time you play the chameleon, you're actually living outside yourself. You're not giving yourself the chance to find out who you are. We've heard so many empaths tell us that as they grew up, they always felt as though they were on the outside looking in. This is why. By not allowing yourself to take that discovery of self, you never learn the energetic lessons presented to you on a timely basis. You miss the opportunity to live a complete life, of living an authentic life. Wouldn't you rather be the sun projecting from within outward, rather than being outside the window, experiencing the storm clouds, with no idea how to come in from the rain?

These lessons are difficult. They're part of the dark path every empath treads on. Yet, it's so vital because these lessons teach you who you are not, opening the way to discover who you are. Instead of trying to fit in by validating others' needs, others' wounds, what if you became the validation simply by your ability to understand what you are capable of? When you validate someone's dysfunctions, you aren't doing them any favors. You're actually giving them permission to continue to wallow in their misery, to not get out of their own way.

In every situation, remember the moments when you were filled with the feelings of peace or love, or without that constriction in your body. Be these memories for others with your own energy. Instead of adding a heavy vibration of shared negativity to try to fit in, be a reminder to others that there is more. Better to be the candle in the dark closet than the wind that blows it out.

The Professionals

3

As Alex struggled to understand what he was experiencing, the dysfunctional energies he was feeling were taking a toll on his physical body. He was plagued with chest pains, headaches, and aches in his joints. He tried his best to ignore them, but it finally got to a point where if he didn't do something, he was never going to survive high school.

Gathering up his courage, he walked into the kitchen, where his mother was preparing dinner, and said, "I can't do this anymore, Mom. There's something wrong with me."

She turned away from the stove and looked into his face. She then put her hand on his forehead. "You don't feel warm."

"I don't have a fever or the flu. It's just that I don't feel right. I think I need to see a doctor."

Alex had never spoken that way to her before, and she became concerned. She quickly called the doctor and made an appointment.

Dr. Dryer was the family physician for as far back as Alex could remember. He was in his early sixties and had a kind, compassionate air about him.

"So, what's wrong, Alex? Your mother sounded very concerned over the phone yesterday," he said as Alex and his mother sat in his office.

"I have headaches; I can't think straight. I don't feel right inside. Sometimes I can't concentrate. I don't feel good in my skin. I feel like I'm sad all the time, and I don't know what to do about it."

"Are you depressed?" Dryer asked.

"I'm not sure."

"Well, do you feel as though nothing is ever going to get better?"

"Right now, I don't know what to think."

"All right, how about feeling a sadness that never seems to leave?"

"Sometimes, but not always."

"How's your appetite?"

"Pretty good, actually."

"Describe to me what you feel."

Alex thought about it for a moment. "Well, sometimes I feel heavy. Like I can't move my arms or legs. I feel emotions that make no sense to me. They pop up out of nowhere. I also feel pains that I can't explain. I just don't feel right inside. I don't even know what feeling good means anymore."

"Tell you what. We'll do some tests to rule out anything physical. How does that sound?"

"That sounds great," Alex's mother replied.

Alex felt hopeful that he'd finally get the answers to understanding what was going on.

He was poked and prodded for the next few days as all sorts of tests were conducted. With each analysis, he found himself praying this would be the test that would tell him what was wrong. He needed answers. He needed to be validated over what he was feeling.

Finally, a week later, the results came in. His mother took the call.

"Alex, it's Dr. Dryer. Thank God there's nothing wrong with you!"

She was happy. Alex was not. His stomach clenched over the possibility that with the tests ruling out a physical cause for his discomfort, it might be something else. Something that had to do with his mental state. Concern now turned to fear.

Now that the physical possibilities had been dealt with, the doctor called Alex and his mother back into his office.

"How are you feeling now?" Dryer asked.

Alex shrugged. "I dunno. I'm having some weird thoughts."

"Weird? In what way?"

Alex felt Dryer's and his mother's alarm at his words. His heart constricted and he found it hard to breathe. He was worried he'd said too much.

"It's hard to explain. Maybe weird isn't the right word."

He looked up and saw that the die had been cast. His use of the word "weird" seemed to set off a red flag.

"I'm going to get you in right away to see a psychiatrist I know," Dryer remarked, plastering what Alex perceived to be a fake smile on his face. "He's very good. I'm sure he'll be able to get to the bottom of what you're feeling."

Alex's stomach immediately tightened. It remained tight as he and his mother walked back to their car.

"I'm sure this new doctor will help you get better," she said a little too brightly as they drove down the road. "You'll be cured, and everything will get back to normal."

I've never felt normal. Alex's stomach clenched even more.

He remained silent on the way home. Once there, he went up to his room to process what he'd been told. Okay, so there was nothing wrong with him physically. As a matter of fact, according to the tests, he was perfectly healthy.

So what was going on? Why was he constantly feeling as though he'd been run over by a truck?

He fumed and fussed and tried his best to figure it out. All he accomplished was making the dull ache in his head worse. Realizing he needed an aspirin, he headed downstairs. Just as he got near the bottom step, he overheard his mother on the phone.

"Oh my God, the doctor thinks Alex is crazy, and wants him to go see a psychiatrist. All I can think about is crazy old Aunt Charlotte. You remember the stories about her, don't you? She was always going on about seeing ghosts, reading people's minds, predicting the future. I don't know what to do. He's my son and I love him, but sometimes he is strange. What if he really is crazy? How in heaven's name am I going to deal with that? How is the family going to deal with that?"

Alex felt the weight of the world crash upon his shoulders as he quietly made his way back up to his room. Is that what had been going on all this time? Was he certifiable? Was he a loon like Aunt Charlotte?

Consumed with fear and dread, despair washed over him. A strange sensation bubbled up inside and he found it difficult to breathe. Terrified, he grabbed his guitar and forced himself to play some chords. They sounded harsh to his ears, but they managed to slowly calm him.

A few days later, he found himself with his mother standing in the waiting room of an office that was painted all white. It reminded him of an insane asylum, which only deepened his anxiety. He immediately felt the need to get out. To forget about this appointment. His stomach ached so badly, he wanted to throw up. He wasn't crazy! And no one was going to tell him he was.

He turned to his mother and was about to demand that they leave when the office door opened and a tall man in his forties stepped out. He wore a pressed suit and glasses.

"I'm Dr. Taylor," he said in a low-pitched, nonemotional voice.

Alex's mother stood up. "Thank you for seeing us," she replied. She started toward the door to his office, only to stop when he held up his hand.

"If you don't mind, I'd like to speak with Alex alone."

A flash of fear played over her face as she looked at her son.

"It's okay, Mom. I'll be fine."

She nodded and sat back down as Alex stood up and followed the doctor into his office. As soon as the door closed behind him and he sat down, he realized the pain in his stomach was easing. As his attention focused on the doctor, he felt a shift. It was hard to admit that he was feeling better. What was different?

He almost gasped aloud when he realized what it might be.

Is it because I'm away from my mother?

"I'd like to gather some background," Dr. Taylor replied before launching into several questions regarding Alex's age, home, school life, etc. Once he was done, he put his pen down and sat back in his chair. He steepled his fingers and quietly regarded Alex over his glasses. "So why do you think you're here, Alex?"

The young man tried his best to formulate a response that wouldn't be perceived as crazy. "There's something wrong," he admitted. "I don't know who I am sometimes. Why I'm overwhelmed with feelings all the time. I get pains, aches. They ran a bunch of tests, and according to them, I'm physically fine. But I don't *feel* fine. I don't know what's going on."

Dr. Taylor remained quiet as he continued to study Alex. Alex in turn forced himself to meet Taylor's eye. He didn't know how, but he felt the doctor's need to discover what was wrong with Alex. It was almost a badge of honor that he uncover what was wrong with the young man sitting across from him.

Was he really tapping into the doctor's thoughts?

As the silence continued between the two, Alex was further surprised to feel the equivalent of Dr. Taylor's fingers probing inside his brain, trying to fathom what was going on. His fear grew as he began to suspect that maybe something really was mentally wrong with him.

The stillness was finally broken when Dr. Taylor asked, "How can I help you get to a better place?"

Despite himself, Alex smiled. "If I knew, I wouldn't be here."

Instantly he felt a jab in his stomach that seemed to come from Dr. Taylor's displeasure at his response, as if Alex had dared to disrespect him with what he perceived to be a smartass remark.

He didn't know what was happening here, but he didn't like it. He couldn't take much more of this. Wild images ran through his brain at the thought that maybe he really was nuts.

Once again it was Dr. Taylor who broke the silence. "In my opinion, I think what you're experiencing are the normal emotional swings that come with puberty. I'm going to put you on a low dosage of medication that will help take the edge off everything you're feeling." He stood up and came around his desk. Approaching Alex, he placed his hand on the young man's shoulder. "We'll talk some more if you want."

No!!!! was what Alex wanted to say. Instead, he mumbled, "Yeah, sure."

The thought of medication managed to calm him. Perhaps the pills would straighten him out and give him that balance he so craved.

When he walked into the outer office, his stomach tightened. Once again, he wondered if what he was feeling was his mother's fears, which were plainly evident on her face.

Is it possible my body has the ability to react to whatever other people are feeling? My mother is terrified that I'm crazy. Her emotions are probably a mess. Is that why my emotions are a mess right now?

They passed by the pharmacy to pick up the medication prescribed by Dr. Taylor. As soon as they got home, he took one and was amazed at how good he felt.

The next morning before he left for school, he took another. It wasn't until he was sitting with his friends in the lunchroom that he suddenly realized the reason he wasn't feeling edgy. The truth was, he wasn't feeling much of *anything*. He was still Alex, but he wasn't the same. He felt as though he was surrounded by a container that nothing could penetrate. Yet, at the same time, he wasn't allowed to penetrate the container—to get out and experience the world around him. He basically felt numb and completely detached. Everything around him felt gray.

Somehow he got through the day. He didn't like feeling emotional, but he hated not feeling anything. One of his friends caught up to him and they walked together toward the bus stop.

"Hey, where were you yesterday?" his friend asked. "We missed you at lunch."

"I had to go see a shrink. I'm not crazy or anything," he quickly added. "But I've been feeling—I dunno."

"Hey, you don't have to explain it to me. I've been seeing a shrink, too. I haven't wanted to say anything; you know how people are. Say, did they give you any meds?"

Alex told him the name of the prescription, and he nodded. "Yeah, I got the same."

"Do you like these pills?"

His friend shrugged. "They keep me from feeling those crazy highs and lows I was experiencing. But at the same time, it's like everything is gray; you know what I mean? I don't get excited over things. It's like I'm just kinda flatlining."

"Are you going to keep taking the pills?"

"Haven't got much of a choice, do I?"

Alex frowned. He hated the thought of living his life in a state of emotionless gray.

There had to be another way. But what was it, and, more importantly, how would he find it?

The **Process**

As we always tell our clients, you have to do what you have to do to feel safe. However, keep in mind that as dark and intense as your journey as an empath is sometimes, it's all part of a process of figuring out who you are. It's an emotional boot camp. If the process is taken away through medication, as in Alex's case, a part of you doesn't feel like you. You go into what we call "a gray place," where you are squeezed into a box energetically, chemically, and emotionally to conform to what others deem as normal. As human beings, we were created to feel, to experience.

It's hard to understand the experience of everyone when your most important sense—which is you—is numb. How will you know how it all fits together if that sense of what, where, how, and why is missing? Your body is a barometer; your mind is a catalog of all your emotional and energetic experiences. In relationships, your sensitivity to energy from others gives you the ability to know if they are being authentic or whether they are sugar coating what they are really feeling. How can you grow and develop a higher truth of emotional experience without your greatest sense—which is the experience of emotions? The choice, ultimately, is up to you. If all the notes of the song are the same, is it truly a song?

The Innocence

4

Alex came out of his musings, startled to find a roomful of students staring back at him. He'd become so wrapped up in his memories, it was as though he'd been physically there, reexperiencing and living through the dark days of high school, learning not only the lessons of the physical world but of the emotional world in his need to survive.

The woman who'd asked him the disruptive question stared at him, enraged that, in her eyes, he'd completely tuned her out. She'd taken a chance to open herself up and he'd ignored her.

"What is wrong with you?" she demanded. "I turn to you for help and you're blowing me off. What kind of a teacher are you?"

Several students immediately jumped to Alex's defense.

"Alex is an excellent teacher!"

"If you'd let him talk, maybe you'd learn something."

And on it went. Alex felt himself losing energetic control of his class. He took a deep breath and turned to her.

"I went through the exact same thing you did. I know what you're going through and what you're experiencing." He looked back to the class. "How many of you have lived through similar situations?"

A few tentatively raised their hands. Then a few more. Soon, the majority of the class had their hands in the air.

"That's what I thought. With your permission, I'm going to change the focus of this class." The students, including the woman, nodded. "Get yourselves comfortable, because I'm going to take you on a journey—my journey. I'm going to share with you how I learned to navigate and survive this dark road that empaths are presented with. Are you ready?" Once again they nodded. "I'll begin with the time when I was in my innocence."

Alex had reached that point in his life that many empaths do—enough is enough. He needed answers and he needed them now.

He was now in college. Through his proficiency with a guitar, he'd joined a band. He felt accepted, liked, even admired. It had gone a long way in building his confidence. However, he was still besieged with feeling waves of everyone's emotions, of feeling so uncomfortable in his own skin that he wanted to scream. Now that he was on a stage, performing before a packed crowd, the anxiety and discomfort grew. He knew it wasn't stage fright. It had to be something else. The fear of having to give up the one thing he truly loved. And that gave him purpose and pushed him to the edge of finding the answers he needed.

It was time to seek out help that had nothing to do with psychiatrists or medical doctors.

One day he was passing the bulletin board in the school cafeteria when a poster caught his attention. There was a large eye staring back at him, advertising "Discover Who You Are at the Moon and the Stars—a holistic store catering to all your metaphysical needs." He wasn't quite sure what a holistic store was or what his metaphysical needs could be, but he certainly wanted to discover who he was. As he studied the poster, he saw photographs of crystals, Tarot cards, candles, and other items. The pictures called to him, though he didn't know why. Feeling he had nothing to lose, he jotted down the address, determined to pay the store a visit. After all, what harm could it do?

Having no classes on the weekend, he decided to visit that upcoming Saturday. The store was only ten minutes away from where he lived, and he could devote as much time as he wanted to exploring the Moon and the Stars.

It was easy to recognize the store. It was in a small strip mall with a large mural of the moon surrounded by a galaxy of stars painted on the large front window. There were a few cars parked outside the door. To his surprise, he felt no trepidation, no sense that what he was doing was wrong. Instead, he was ready to walk through the front door and enter a world he knew nothing about.

There were several displays near the entrance. He was immediately drawn to a set of what looked like Native American drums. Nearby was a table with an array of various crystals of all shapes and sizes. As he took a breath, his lungs were filled with the welcoming scent of sandalwood incense.

This place somehow knows who I am, he realized to himself as he slowly made his way up and down the aisles, past the Tarot decks, books, jewelry, and other things that looked intriguing.

The more he browsed, the more he began to sense what could be described only as an energy that draped itself over him—like a warm comforter. Yet, it wouldn't be until later that he realized that beneath this energy there lurked something not quite right—as if the comforter could, at any moment, draw itself down over his face and suffocate him.

He rounded the corner and saw a man standing behind the register. He was short and a little on the heavy side. He had dark-brown hair and a graying beard. His eyes, though, were a startling blue. Alex met his gaze and inwardly shivered. He instantly felt as though this man had the ability to see right through him.

He smiled at Alex. "I'm Germaine. Is there anything I can help you with?"

His voice was low and melodious and managed to calm any anxiety Alex may have felt being in an unfamiliar place.

"I was just curious, that's all. I'm afraid I don't know much about all this holistic stuff."

Once again Germaine's eyes met Alex's. "You've had some experiences you can't explain, haven't you?"

Alex gave a start. "How did you know?" he blurted out.

"You've come to the right place. We have seminars, healings, and readings here that are geared to helping you find the answers you're looking for. And bring you energetically to a better place."

Alex was astounded by the man's words. A surge of hope shot through him. "You mean, I don't need to go out in nature to get to that better place?"

Germaine laughed. "Nature is wonderful for that. But I can teach you how to do it no matter where you are. You could be standing in the middle of a crowd at rush hour in the busiest city in the world, and you can still feel balanced and unaffected by what's going on around you."

My God! This is exactly what I've been looking for!

"Do you have any information on that?" Alex eagerly asked.

Germaine leaned under the counter and produced a few pamphlets. "Here, read these. It will explain all we do here."

Alex took them, thanked Germaine for his time, and went home. He was no sooner through the front door than he began to study the pamphlets the man had given him.

There was one in particular that called to him. Above a picture that featured a circle of chairs surrounding a white candle and crystals, the caption read, "A Gathering of Like-Minded People—Understanding Why You're Different. Discover Who You Truly Are."

Alex smiled. If this seminar wasn't for him, nothing was.

The seminar was for the following Saturday evening. He called, signed himself up, and waited eagerly for the day to arrive.

As he drove to the Moon and the Stars, he'd made up his mind that he was simply going there to observe. He wasn't ready to share anything of himself. He knew there were degrees of being different, and he wasn't about to share his life's story if these people were either slightly different or beyond-the-chasm different.

At the same time, he arrived without any agenda. Without intention. Almost as if he was in a state of innocence. All he brought with him that night was a deep sense of curiosity.

The room was in the back of the store, surprising Alex with its large size. There were chairs set up much like the picture on the brochure. In the center of the chairs, on the floor, was a white pillar candle. Surrounding it were crystals of all shapes and sizes.

Alex immediately noticed there were more women than men in the group. It was easy to see he was the youngest—all the participants ranged in age from late thirties to early sixties. He also noticed the intensity of the energy in the room. There didn't seem to be any rhyme or rhythm to what he was feeling, yet there was more energy here than he usually felt in his everyday life. That alone intrigued him.

Germaine swept into the room and took his place behind one of the chairs. "Thank you all for coming. We're here to share and discuss. To find out where each of you is on the energetic spectrum."

Alex felt a fear rush through him. This put a different spin on things. He hadn't planned on discussing. And he certainly hadn't planned on sharing. Anxiety kicked in.

He glanced behind him and wondered if he could make it to the door without being seen. But there were too many people. And through the fear, he began to feel the force of their energy. Once again he realized he was feeling more energy from them than he normally felt from his friends and fellow students. He sensed their need to find out who they are. It was the same need he had.

"I'd like you all to understand how powerful you really are," Germaine continued. "You underestimate your energy. And how you can use that energy to affect world events. The political scene. The environment. Do you want to save the planet? Of course you do. And you can!"

The last of Germaine's words hit Alex squarely in his gut. He'd been able to go along with what the man was saying until he uttered the need to save the planet. He immediately felt that yucky feeling crawl all over him. It didn't make sense. Who didn't want to save the planet? But he couldn't reconcile the words he was hearing with what he was physically feeling.

In his innocence, he decided to stay and try to figure this out.

A woman abruptly stood up. She was dressed in an aqua-colored caftan, and she wore an abundance of bead necklaces around her neck that shook whenever she moved.

"My name is Mystic Gaia. I'd like to bring everyone's attention to what's going on in the Amazon rainforest. The businesses are destroying the environment. They're murdering the indigenous population in their insatiable need to rape and destroy the forest in order to line their pockets. We need to do something about it. We should do a circle and send all the love and energy we can down there so the businesses will realize what they're doing and stop."

Alex eyed the woman. He wasn't sure about her name, nor about what she wanted to do. Once again, it didn't quite feel right to him. At the same time, he knew he was here to learn. Maybe there was merit to what she was saying and what she wanted to do. He loved the planet—the forests, the animals. Maybe she had a point. Not knowing enough about any of this, who was he to question it?

He stood up and was physically and energetically pulled into the circle. As the woman began to intone a prayer, he found himself opening up. And feeling that rare feeling that he'd found a place where he could belong. Even though the people's energy still felt a little wonky, it was still better than what he was accustomed to feeling in his daily life.

By the time he left, he felt wonderful. Almost drunk. It was as if he could walk on air. Yet, the farther he moved away from the store, the energies of the evening began to dissipate, leaving him with an all-too-familiar heaviness.

Arriving home and lying on the couch, he thought about the evening. And tried to analyze why he'd felt so high and almost drunk with giddiness at the store, yet the farther away he got from the store, the energy turned heavier.

Was it possible he'd pulled himself deeper into the group's energy by aligning himself with their beliefs, their energy, and, yes, even their power? Much as he had done in high school when he was the chameleon?

He continued to ponder it. As he did so, his eyelids grew heavy. Before he knew what was happening, he fell asleep.

He found himself in the rainforest. He watched as the trees were mowed down by bulldozers. The mighty Amazon River was awash in black, gelatinous oil. Somehow he was able to simply witness what he was seeing, without plugging into the wanton destruction around him. Above the noise of the bulldozer, he heard a voice. "It will be all right. Find your place and know that every place would want you to be with them."

He awoke with a start. What the hell was that?

As he rubbed his eyes, he thought back to the dream. What did it mean? What had the voice meant? It was too strange to contemplate.

Alex got up and went to bed. For the next week, he went about his life, going to classes, studying, practicing his guitar. Then came the night for the next meeting at the Moon and the Stars.

It was the same group of people who'd attended the last meeting. This time, a man stood up and urged all of them to write letters to stop the hunting of whales. He became almost hysterical as he described, in detail, the slaughter of these majestic animals.

When it came time to do the prayer circle, Alex didn't have the same experience he'd had at the previous meeting. Everything felt different—the energy of the circle, the energy of the prayers. The energy actually felt *heavier* than the week before. He couldn't understand it. He loved whales and didn't want to see them mercilessly hunted down. Yet, none of this felt good.

Alex felt overwhelmed. He stepped back from the circle and tried to shrug it off. It was difficult though.

"I need to go," he blurted out as the unease in his body increased. He took a few steps toward the door when Germaine stopped him.

"You don't need to leave," the man said. "You're an important member of this group. We'd all like you to stay."

"I'd like to, but I'm tired. And feeling a bit off. What you're doing is great; don't get me wrong. I love whales. Maybe I'm coming down with something."

Mystic Gaia spoke up. "Alex, you're the youngest one in our group. This planet is going to be yours someday. You need to stay and participate. You need to put your own energy into what we're doing so the world you inherit isn't completely screwed up."

What she said made sense. He did have an obligation to do all he could to save the planet. Her attention calmed him. He allowed himself to be led back into the circle. The prayers continued. So did the heaviness in Alex's heart. As the words became more militaristic, more imbued with rage, Alex's chest constricted, as if he was having a heart attack. He prayed for this circle to finally end. When it did, he headed straight for the door. He couldn't wait to escape this overwhelming ache in his heart.

Just as he reached the door, he felt a hand on his shoulder. Turning, he found himself face to face with Germaine.

"I'm glad you decided to stick it out." Alex nodded but said nothing. "I actually wanted to speak with you. You see, there's much that I can teach you if you're willing. Tell me, what do you know about crystals?"

Alex's attention was immediately riveted to Germaine's words, the ache in his heart easing. "I know I feel things from them," he admitted.

"That's perfect. Do you know why you feel things from crystals?"

Alex shook his head. "Not really."

"Crystals are considered the bones of the earth. They hold information and energy to help us. They have the ability to make us more powerful, to open up channels. They allow us to work in partnership with them in order to gain all the knowledge they want to pass down to us. It just so happens that working with stones and crystals is my specialty."

His heaviness disappeared as he was sucked into Germaine's interest in him. "Whenever I hike the mountains and sit on the rocks, they make me feel wonderful. Maybe there is something to all of this."

Germaine grinned. "Of course there is. And I'd be more than happy to sit and chat with you at our next meeting."

Alex once again felt hopeful that he was about to receive the answers he'd been looking for. And from an experienced teacher no less. His energy shifted from heaviness to almost giddy. Yet, just as before, the farther away he got from the store, the more the lighter energy disappeared, replaced with an uneasiness he couldn't quite understand.

By the time he arrived home, he felt completely drained. He quickly washed up, threw off his clothes, and jumped into bed. Even before his head hit the pillow, he was asleep.

This time, he dreamed he was sitting atop his favorite mountain. Looking at his feet, he was astonished to see waves of muddy-looking energy draining out of him. The more this energy drained out of him, the lighter he felt.

"Everyone is going to want you to be in their circle." Alex whipped his head around, trying to find the owner of the voice. "But the mountain doesn't ask you to be anyone but yourself."

Alex awoke the next morning, the dream stuck in his head. Once again he pondered the words of the disembodied voice and the feeling that he'd actually been on his favorite mountain.

He went to school, trying his best to pay attention to his classes, even as his mind reeled with what had been happening lately, especially in the dreamtime. These dreams seemed to have been triggered by his attendance at the meetings at the Moon and the Stars.

What was it about this Germaine guy that could cause him to have such wacky dreams? And affect his energy simply by paying attention to him? And what exactly did Germaine want to teach him?

Part of him knew he should just chuck the idea of returning to the holistic store. Yet, another part pulled at him, dangling the hope in front of him like a golden carrot that he'd finally understand why he was so different.

At the end of the day, he had no choice. He had to go back. He had to find out why he felt all that he felt.

And so the teaching began.

The **Teaching** Begins

Throughout your life as an empath, especially in the beginning, you have absolutely no frame of reference of what you're feeling or how to gauge your own emotional state. You believe you have no choice but to become accustomed to hearing "you're too sensitive" or "you're too emotional." You grab onto anything that will provide that frame of reference needed to navigate your life. Somewhere along the line, something that resonates with you grabs your attention. This begins the journey into the rabbit hole of learning who and what this energy is and why you are the way you are. The problem is, there are hundreds of explanations for what this idea of energy is. Everywhere you turn, there are elucidations from the religious community, the New Age community, the pagan community, etc. They all have the answer for what the ideal experience of this energy you're feeling is. Not only from the beginning, but for the rest of your life. But who really has the answer?

Because many empaths hide away or downplay what they feel, in the beginning of their path there is an innocence, a vulnerability, an inability to really judge anything outside of themselves. Because once you judge, the act of judging changes the energy around you. Even if you don't quite understand your role in changing the energy by judging it, you still end up becoming your own worst enemy. In your vulnerability to have some kind of understanding, you reach out, looking for answers. This is where many fall prey to those who take advantage of an empath's innocence.

What you as an empath forget, or may not even know, is how powerful you are and why you attract these types of people just waiting to take advantage of you. You are a feeler, a seer, a healer. One hopes that someday, you will come to understand all these aspects of the energy that come to you. Many people who put themselves out there as teachers aren't quite at that level. They may have knowledge but have become addicted to the energy of the new student to use according to their own agenda. It's up to you to learn to discern—to listen to what the energy is telling you. Even fledging empaths know what energy feels like; whether it makes them feel good or makes them feel heavy. You must learn to listen to that energy whenever you are presented with a new teacher or a new thought process. Only by listening to your own gift of empathy will you be able to pick through the many teachers in order to find the right one. How will you know when you've found the right one? You will FEEL it. Real teachers become filled with energy from a higher source because they are part of the energetic solution, not the energetic problem. The knowledge they share will resonate with you. No matter how famous or obscure the teacher is, always trust what you feel. It's there for a reason.

Everything is an energetic cue that is teaching you who you are and your energetic role in life. Never forget that the dark road also teaches. Many times even the experience of discomfort energetically is overcome by a curiosity or an unseen inner voice that pushes you past your discomfort. All this is a lesson in understanding your energetic radar.

Nighttime
Rendezvous

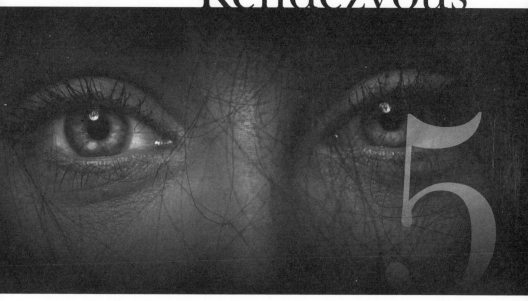

5

Suddenly Alex had a teacher. Someone who had taken him under his wing. Someone who could explain all the things Alex had been feeling his entire life, but never understanding. He was excited, grateful that he was finally going to comprehend why he was the way he was. In his excitement, he pointedly ignored the heaviness he sometimes felt around Germaine. He chalked it up to his own innate shyness. He wasn't accustomed to opening up to anyone about the over-the-top experiences he'd gone through. He wasn't one of those types who wore his emotions on his sleeve. So he pushed aside the tugging in his belly that warned him to be careful, and plunged headlong into grabbing onto all the information Germaine was willing to impart.

Every Saturday night, Alex went to the meetings. There was now a shift. The group no longer seemed concerned with saving the rainforest, or the whales, or changing the government in Washington, DC. The meetings now became about the individual and what he or she had personally experienced.

"I want you all to feel the energy in this room. It's incredibly powerful, isn't it?" Germaine smiled. People nodded. Alex felt a tug— an intangible sense of something he couldn't quite explain yet. But he nodded anyway. "Do you know what's amazing about this powerful energy? It's all coming from you. That's right. It's coming from each and every one of you."

As Germaine said this, he looked directly at Alex, who gulped in astonishment.

"We're going to do a guided meditation. Is there anyone here who has never done a guided meditation?" Alex sheepishly raised his hand. "Don't worry, my boy. It's quite simple. You're going to close your eyes and listen to my words. You and everyone here will have an experience. And this experience will have an intention, which we will discuss afterward. Now, everyone get comfortable." Germaine produced a drum from behind his chair. "It's been proven that the sound of a gentle drumbeat induces your mind to relax, to go into a meditative state. As I drum, listen to my words and see where it takes you."

Alex slumped down in his chair and closed his eyes. He'd never experienced this before and wondered just what was about to happen. He took a deep breath and let it out. The drumming began.

He was amazed to find his body reacting to the drum, his heartbeat syncing up with each rhythmic beat. As Germaine struck the animal hide and the room resonated with the sound, the young man felt his tension release and his body relax.

"I am Germaine. I am the keeper of this journey. I stand here before you. Listen to my drum. As I create the sound from my drum, I ask each of you to let go and open up to me. Know that when you open up to me, I know the power flows through me to you."

Alex felt almost inebriated. He felt his energy being pulled back and forth as though someone were blowing air into him, then releasing the air from his body a few moments later. It was blissful. And intoxicating. It continued on until all Alex could see, through closed eyes, was Germaine's face in front of him. There was nothing else but Germaine. No other experiences, no other visions, and no other energies but that of Germaine's.

Alex didn't know how long the meditation lasted. Germaine's words danced around him, pulling at him as he found himself floating above the room, his spirit hovering over the group.

Just as he felt he could drift through the ceiling and out into the night air, the drumming abruptly stopped. Alex felt himself jarringly yanked back into his body. Opening his eyes as he sat up, he felt unnaturally lethargic. As if it cost him to move his limbs. He glanced at Germaine, astonished at how this journey had affected his sense of self. Was that normal? He looked around to see if anyone else experienced what he'd experienced. As usual, everyone looked fine. Some even looked charged up.

Damn it. Why do I always feel as though I'm out of step with everyone else?

As everyone clamored about how amazing the meditation had been, Germaine approached Alex. "How did you do?" he asked, his blue eyes intently watching the young man.

He lifted his shoulders, still struggling to understand what he'd just experienced. Not sure what to think yet, he answered, "It was cool," as politely as he could, reluctant to offend the man he was beginning to think of as a mentor.

"Don't worry, Alex. It's a learned practice. You just need to let go more. Relax. Let it in and get out of your worries. You'll soon be just as good as the rest of us."

As Alex made his way home, he felt confused. Things weren't quite adding up. He couldn't shake the unease whenever he remembered how Germaine's energy had affected him. As if the man had actually been able to go in and pull Alex's energy from him. The rest of the group didn't seem to have experienced that at all. He didn't know much about meditation, but he did know that it was supposed to invigorate you, not drain you. Yet, he felt as though someone had opened up a hole in the soles of his feet that allowed his energy to seep out of him. What happened? It was obvious Germaine was a pretty powerful guy. Was it possible he'd used that power to take what he wanted from Alex? Why?

He couldn't wrap his mind around it all. A nagging sensation kept at him. All he knew was that he hoped his misgivings were wrong. The man was a teacher. Surely he couldn't be that manipulative?

When Alex went to bed that night, he instantly fell asleep. Instead of dreaming of his favorite mountain, or the Amazon rainforest, he dreamed of Germaine. Lying in his bed, he saw Germaine standing at the footboard.

"Come with me, Alex," Germaine said as he beckoned to Alex. With each wave of his hand, Alex's energy dipped and drained. He suddenly felt a shiver of fear run through him. He'd seen this before in the old *Dracula* movie, when Bela Lugosi terrifyingly whispered to helpless humans to come to him. Everyone knew what happened when Bela's whisper was obeyed. Was Germaine a vampire?

Overcome with horror, Alex knew he had to break the connection. To stop this intrusion of his energy from being drained away until he was left with nothing. Digging deep down inside, he found the courage to yell out, "Stop!"

Instantly, he awoke to find himself alone in his room. He pulled a trembling hand through his hair as he tried to calm his galloping heart.

Trying to convince himself it was just a dream, Alex got up and padded into the living room, where he spent the rest of the night watching old movies. The dream retreated but the fear lingered.

The next morning as he sat in class, he was unnerved by the sight of Germaine's face disrupting his concentration. No matter what he did, the man's face continued to intrude into his thoughts. Each time it did, he felt the drain on his energy. At first he was frightened. But as it went on, his fear turned to anger. This was crazy! Why was Germaine doing this to him? He'd done nothing except search for answers.

His anger and frustration grew. After two days of this, he drove to the store, determined to have it out with Germaine. It was one thing to serve as his teacher; it was quite another to interfere with his daily life.

Walking through the front door, his resentment empowered him. One way or the other, he was going to get to the bottom of why each time he had the vision of Germaine, his energy was adversely affected.

Germaine looked up from the register as Alex walked in. "Hey, Alex. How are you doing?" he asked, his mouth upturned in a welcoming smile. However, it was the expression in his eyes and the energy of how he held himself that immediately caught Alex's attention. It was the look and feel of a man who knew he held a secret that the other wanted. A secret that gave him superiority over Alex.

"Actually, I'm not doing too well," Alex said.

"Why? What's the matter?"

"I'm feeling drained out and heavy. And I think it's because of you."

To his surprise, rather than take offense, Germaine chuckled. "Took you long enough to figure it out."

"What?" Alex remarked, startled by the man's casual admission.

"Remember the meditation we did the other night?" Alex nodded. "I deliberately entered your thoughts and manipulated your energy. In fact, I've been doing that for the past two days."

"Why would you do that?"

"To see if you could pick up on the fact that I attached a cord to you."

Alex's heart began to hammer. "What's a cord?" he asked, not sure he wanted to hear the response, but knowing he had to.

"It happens all the time. People with power or lack of power can at times pull energy from others. Sometimes it's done intentionally.

Sometimes, it isn't. Some can even do it in dreams. Each time you react to something, whether through anger, sadness, etc., you release your energy. Those who know how, take that energy. It drains you and empowers them. People learn your energetic triggers. When they do, let the draining begin," he chuckled.

This angered Alex. But it also made sense.

This hadn't just happened with Germaine. He thought back to all those people he'd known who'd popped into his mind for no reason at all or appeared in his dreams. Or, like the bullies in high school, who upset him enough that he reacted in a negative way. He always felt drained after these events occurred.

"That's—that's diabolical!" Alex exclaimed.

"No. It's part of being a human being. We all take from each other. Sometimes we give. But mostly we take. Some not even realizing how their neediness drains the people around them."

Alex grew angrier. It was the strong preying on the weak. The weak exploiting the kindness of the caring individual. People everywhere feeding from this energy. Taking advantage and manipulating from a perceived need, whether they knew what they were doing or not. It was part of what made this world so difficult to live in. His anger intensified—so much so that it was starting to take him over. He knew that if he let it go too far, he'd never be able to rein it back. He glanced at Germaine and saw his smile. And instantly understood it. If he continued to let the anger grow, Germaine was ready to lap it up.

He'd be damned if he let that happen.

He took a long, deep, steadying breath and pulled the anger back.

"What are we going to do about it?" he demanded.

"What are *you* going to do about it?" Germaine countered.

"What's that supposed to mean? I came here looking for answers. You've acted like you're my friend, my teacher. What you're doing isn't fair."

Germaine shrugged his shoulders. "Get used to it, kid. Everything has a payment. How better to teach you than to show you what it feels like to be drained?"

"How do I stop it?" Alex asked.

"What's it worth to you?"

Alex's simmering anger instantly turned to fear. Its icy fingers wound their way around his heart as he whispered, "It's worth everything to me, but I don't have anything."

Germaine grinned at him. In that moment, Alex realized he'd been duped. His innocence and eagerness to learn had overshadowed the unease he'd felt when he'd first met Germaine. His own naiveté precluded him from picking up on the insidious intention that was now making itself perfectly clear.

He found himself sinking down into that dark place inside himself. The place where doubt and self-loathing and the realization that he'd never fit in resided.

Germaine saw the expression on his face and laughed. "Come on, Alex. I was just joking with you. Don't look so damned glum. Work with me some more. There's something you can do that many can't. I want to figure out what makes you tick. Do you want me to be your teacher for real?"

"Is that the payment you were talking about?"

"You always have a choice. You can go back to the way you were. Or you can continue on."

Alex hesitated. He hated being made the fool. But this man had power. And knowledge. Could he push aside his own misgivings to gain access to this knowledge?

"I need to figure this all out," he replied.

Germaine nodded. "All right. We continue on. Come see me in a couple of days. In the meantime, I'll cut the cord and stop visiting you in the dreamtime."

Alex frowned. "How do you cut the cord?"

The man lifted his eyes and met Alex's. A malevolent smile played across his lips. "You'll see."

Vulnerability

As an empath, you have the ability to quickly sense the lows and the highs of where energy is. Sometimes it seems as though the lows and the highs are all you have. The middle ground doesn't seem to work anymore. Even as you crave normalcy, it is the highs and the lows that start the process of learning who you are. This intensity pushes you onward on your journey of learning what it means to be an empath.

As you begin the learning process, you are understandably vulnerable. Unfortunately, there are people who will take advantage of that vulnerability. It is no different from predators out in the wild. They seek out the weak on which to pounce. But does that not also teach the prey to become more clever in order to escape the predator?

There are many terms for people who have the ability to drain you of your energy. A popular one is "energy vampire." They will attach a cord to you. They will then make demands, promises, whatever it takes to elicit a response from you. Because you are so desperate to be okay, you are prey to those who recognize your desperate need to be okay. How many times have people come up to you and, knowing how sensitive you are, say something to elicit a response from you? In that moment when you let your guard down, because you're angry or hurt, they plug into you. They connect that cord. And the draining of your energy begins.

Think back to those times when a friend comes to you and dumps all their troubles on you. You empathize with them and the cord finds its way in. We all have friends who fall into the practice of "poor me" to get energy from others.

It's not difficult to cut cords. However, you could be cutting cords all day. Is there another way?

The trick is to understand what is going on. To feel that initial pull on your energy. One way you can stop this from happening is by refusing to let your energy be pulled from you. There is a way to go neutral with your energy—a change of thought that you will not allow anyone to take your energy from you. Another is to constantly put up some kind of energetic protection. Yet another is to find where the intrusion of the cord is in your belly; envision cutting it off with a knife or sword and sending it back without judgment (once you judge, the cord is automatically attached). However, this entails a constant vigil to keep yourself protected or by cutting the cords each time they attach.

What if this is giving you a bigger understanding of your personal power? It's about recognizing and learning your energetic triggers—those buttons that others know how to push in you that get you to react—that create the opening that allows the energetic connection to be made. It takes practice. And you will falter. But if you continue the learning process, you will come out ahead. You will no longer be the prey animal to an energy vampire. One of the most important lessons to learn is that **no one can take your energy from you unless you allow it.** Learn your triggers. Learn how they affect you. Once you do that, you can begin to experience the empowerment in becoming a confident presence to those who wish to learn from you instead of taking from you.

Envy

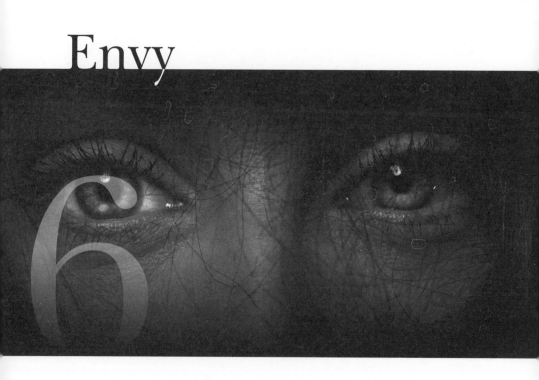

Alex felt himself between a rock and a hard place. As much as he loathed how much Germaine had taken advantage of his naiveté, he nevertheless knew he could learn much from the man. He knew of no one else who could teach him what he needed to know.

If he was making a deal with the devil, at least he was entering it with open eyes. After all, Germaine did seem to understand what he'd been going through his entire life. And his shop did pop up when he was at the end of his rope.

He therefore spent the next few months attending the meetings and learning what he could about energy. During the meditations, he began to experience what he could describe only as vivid visions. Animals began to play a large part in those visions. Not sure if he could yet totally trust Germaine, he instead went to the library and looked up animal imagery. He discovered there was a tradition, going back to the beginnings of mankind, in which animals played a huge part in the mystical beliefs of human beings.

As winter slowly turned into spring, Alex began to have visions of deer, both male and female. He wasn't sure what the visions meant, but as he'd been learning, the meaning would be revealed in its own time.

It was a beautiful morning. The temperatures were finally letting go of the cold briskness and turning into warm breezes that promised summer was just around the corner. Driving to school, he turned the corner and felt his heart sink when he saw a dead buck lying on the side of the road. He'd been developing a deepening affinity with animals, and it saddened him to see this beautiful animal's lifeless body. Thanks to the weekly meetings, he'd been learning about blessings and thought to do a little prayer for the spirit of the buck. The animal's life had to mean something more than just ending up as a carcass on the side of the road.

Pulling over, he climbed out of his car and slowly approached the deer. He stood over the animal, closed his eyes, and began to recite words that came from his heart. "I'm so sorry this happened to you," he whispered under his breath. "I really hope you're in a better place. People never seem to pay attention when they drive. Accept this humble offering of words from someone who really wishes we all could live together without harm."

Suddenly, in that moment, he felt an energy he'd never felt before whoosh through him. There was a purity to it that left him breathless. Opening his eyes, he was astonished to see the spirit of the deer standing before him. He didn't know what to say. Or do. He just stood and stared at the spirit. "Oh my God," he replied. "Is this real?"

In his excitement, he wondered if he should try harder to honor the woodland spirit of the deer. In a need to do more, he closed his eyes again. "I'm sure you're upset that you lost your life. You're so majestic and I thank you for appearing to me. I hope you can now move on. I'll try harder to understand what your life and death can teach us all."

Alex opened his eyes again. The deer spirit was still there. He was about to despair that he'd done the blessing all wrong when the spirit of the deer moved toward him. As he froze in astonishment, the deer bowed, his antlers almost touching the ground, as if acknowledging a shared existence with the human who stood before him.

Suddenly and unexpectedly, the deer then stepped *into* Alex.

His energy instantly changed. At first he wasn't quite sure what was happening. But through his confusion, it dawned on him that somehow, someway, he was actually becoming the deer. He'd read about this process. It was called shapeshifting, and it was a practice many shamans undertook to strengthen the tie between themselves and the animal world.

He looked around at the woods, tingling, full of warmth, as if his energy was being elevated. The colors of the trees became sharper. More distinct. He suddenly heard sounds he'd never heard before. He felt as though he could taste the wind as it danced across his skin. His senses were more acute, more alive. It was so profound, so awe inspiring; there were no words to describe what he was experiencing.

"I love this!" he shouted. "Thank you," he added, knowing the deer had given him an unimaginable gift. He jumped into his car and drove straight to the store—the only place he thought his experience would be understood and appreciated. He ran in and found Germaine at the register. "You're not going to believe what just happened to me!" He blurted out his experience, giddily recounting, as best he could, the energy he'd felt when the deer stepped into him.

"You don't need that," Germaine snapped when Alex was done. He snatched up a crystal from the display case and put it on Alex's heart, and the energy of the deer instantly disappeared.

Alex felt as though he'd tumbled off a high cliff. "Why did you do that?" he asked in disbelief.

"That's foolishness. You don't need that," he repeated.

"What are you talking about? That's probably the best I've ever felt in my entire life!"

"You're not supposed to be doing stuff on your own. You do only what I tell you to do."

Alex stared at his teacher. A knowing crept over him, a knowing that left him aghast.

Germaine was envious.

Alex had just done something that Germaine had never done. And probably couldn't do. He'd had an experience Germaine could never begin to comprehend.

He didn't know what to make of that. He hadn't deliberately set out to experience what he did. It had happened all on its own. His words and prayer had created a gift of his heart to the deer, which the deer in turn had reciprocated with a gift of its own. Yet, Germaine was accusing him of doing something wrong. Of somehow disrespecting him.

Alex felt so deflated that he didn't know what to do. Or say. So he turned around and quietly left the store.

Victimhood

There are many people out there who have spent years and a great deal of money developing skills that allow them to feel special in a competitive world of who can and can't do what. Empaths come to this world with all those abilities—the ability to see, to sense, to understand energy. These gifts are what make up what we call an energetic experience. As it was with Alex, sometimes it takes an energetic experience to push us forward on our spiritual path.

What Alex experienced with the deer is a wonderful introduction to the wonders of the natural world and, more importantly, realizing we are not separate from the animals, the trees, the stones, etc. This is the reason that animals are attracted to empaths. Just as they have a sensitivity to their surroundings, so do empaths. In that shared kindred experience, they are attracted to us and strive to help us with the learning of our gift, whether in spirit as a totem animal or as a live animal.

Whereas animals try to teach, humans use energetic triggers to compete from places of fear. Our human relationships go awry. As an empath, how many times have you experienced someone pooh-poohing something you like to do or crave or have accomplished? How fast did your energy drain out of you? This is the gift of that dark moment. You don't need to be the victim. You don't need to believe their negative thoughts regarding you. Victimhood becomes a judgment of self that goes so deep into our energetic system, it's almost impossible to stop once it begins. All the negative beliefs and thoughts that are lurking within suddenly become empowered and heavier, taking on a false truth of the meaning we give them. That false truth is like a faucet. It is now open. These energies of judgment flow from us, draining us.

As hard as it is to experience that, know that it's a lesson that needs to be learned in order to recognize the difference between being empowered and disempowered. Without the understanding that these moments are valuable learning opportunities, many empaths immediately go into victimhood. As we know, victimhood only drains you of your energy. It never empowers; it disempowers. It stops you on your path of self-discovery. Know that these lessons—difficult as they are—are teaching you to be stronger. To use the late Princess Diana as an example, for many years she believed herself to be the victim of what she called "the Establishment." But as she grew older, she learned to stop being the victim—she empowered herself by leaving that victim energy behind and moving forward on the path she'd set out for herself. It's a shining example of what we're all capable of once we change our mindset from being a victim to being a confident person with a right to be here.

The Search

The woman's irritated voice interrupted Alex as he looked around the classroom. "Your stories are entertaining. But they're not telling me how to deal with what I'm seeing and experiencing. Are you going to help me or not?"

Alex recognized her desperation. He met her eye and smiled. "I've been where you are. I've asked the same questions you're asking. Bear with me. I will help you."

Alex now knew that the answers he'd been seeking did not lie with Germaine. He'd felt the man's envy, his need to keep Alex firmly under his thumb. He may still have a lot to learn, but he knew enough that Germaine's way was not the right way for him.

Despite being disappointed in how it all had turned out, he at least felt proud that he hadn't let his anger get the best of him. He felt comforted that he'd learned something valuable in what could otherwise be construed of as a negative experience.

However, it was time to move on. To expand his search to discover who he was and what this energy Germaine spoke of was all about.

Once again he delved into a variety of books in an effort to understand why he was the way he was. One afternoon, while he was having lunch in the cafeteria, he had his nose buried in a book. It was propped up in front of him, and it spoke of different traditions in the world of mysticism. They spoke of energies, visions, ceremonies, and rituals designed to elicit an otherworldly experience. He was so engrossed that he didn't notice the young woman who slid into the chair opposite him. It wasn't until she gently banged her lunch tray on the table that he looked up.

He recognized her. She was in his sociology and English lit classes. His heart began to beat faster. She was cute, with long blonde hair, a dimple in her chin, and the deepest green eyes he'd ever seen. He'd been attracted to her from the first moment he saw her, but he lacked the courage to approach. Now here she was.

"Hey Alex."

"Hey Angela."

"I don't recall that book you're reading being assigned in any of our classes." He could see she was teasing him. Not wanting her to think he was weird, he picked the book up, closed it and shoved it under his other stack of school books. "Oh, don't hide it. I came over because I wanted to let you know I'd read it, too."

His eyes widened in surprise. "You did?"

She nodded. "Uh huh. Lots of my friends are reading it. Don't bother finishing it though. It was just okay." She reached for her soda and took a sip. "The truth is, it didn't really explain why I feel the things I do."

Alex was flabbergasted. The girl of his dreams was experiencing the same things he was? Was it possible?

"You feel these weird things too? Wow."

"I wish I could find a place or a teacher that could answer all the questions I have."

Alex nodded. "I know what you mean. I thought I'd found such a place, but the guy just took advantage of me."

"What place is that?"

"The Moon and the Stars over on Grant Street."

Angela laughed. "Oh my God, that Germaine is a total creep. He tried to lure me in the same way. Said he wanted to teach me, blah blah blah. But after two meetings I got the hell out of there. I always felt as though I'd been slimed every time I left there." She leaned forward. "Actually, I think I may have found a place that has answers for the both of us. It's about a half hour from here, but I've heard good things about it. It's called the Angelic Church of Mysticism."

"Church?" he asked dubiously.

"Don't worry. I don't think it's that kind of a church with priests and all that. Say, why don't we go together this Saturday night? They're having a get-together. We can check it out, if you're game."

Alex was over the moon. Not only was there finally the possibility that he'd find what he was after, but he'd be doing it in the company of a beautiful girl.

What could go wrong with that winning combination?

"I'm definitely game."

He could hardly wait for Saturday to arrive. When it did, he met Angela on campus. She got into his car and they drove to the address she'd provided.

The Angelic Church of Mysticism turned out to be a medium-sized one-floor building tucked in among residential homes. Pulling up, they saw that the small parking lot was already full. Alex managed to squeeze his car in between two other vehicles. They got out and looked to the building, then to each other.

"How does it feel to you?" Angela asked.

"Not too bad. How about you?"

"I agree. Not too bad. Yet." She laughed as she said this. "Wow, look at us. We've developed some kind of feeling radar together."

He beamed at her words. Together, the two young people walked around to the back of the building, where a door was propped open. Entering, the room opened up to what looked like a regular church. There were pews with a podium at the front. In the back of the room there was a long table on which food and drinks were laid out. There were about thirty people milling about, engaged in quiet conversations as they ate and drank.

The two stayed close as they walked farther into the room. Two women who looked to be in their late twenties detached themselves from one of the groups and came over.

"Welcome! My name is Brenda, and this is my friend Sue." Alex and Angela introduced themselves. "So happy you two could make it tonight. This is a place where people come to be found."

"Well, I'd love to have some kind of knowing of who I am and why I'm going through what I'm going through," Angela piped up.

"What are you going through?"

She pointed to Alex. "The same thing he is. Crazy things that we'd like to more fully understand."

"We believe in doing what we call blessings," Brenda explained. "There are people here who have done a great deal of inner work and healing on themselves. Because of that, they have the ability to bestow blessings on those who haven't done the work yet. The blessings bring you to a knowing of who you are. It's a very conscious action experience that will make you feel better." She turned to Alex. "Do you mind if we do a blessing on you?"

It had been a long time since Alex had felt anything resembling better. Anything was worth a shot at this point. "Sure, I'll give it a try."

"I'll go with you," Angela said.

Brenda held up her hand. "In order for this to be effective, it has to be a private experience."

Angela took a step back. "Sure, no problem. I'll just mingle around out here. Have fun, Alex."

He hesitated, wondering just what he was getting into. But Angela had already returned to the table, and the two women were beckoning him to follow. *Here goes nothing*, he thought as they walked up to the podium. There was a curtain off to the right and they led him there. Pushing aside the curtains, he found himself in a small room. A tall file cabinet sat in the corner, while a solitary chair was placed in the middle of the area.

"You can sit there, Alex," Brenda said.

As Alex sat down, he watched as Brenda crossed over to the filing cabinet. She opened up the drawer and took out an 8-by-10 manila envelope. She opened it and withdrew two white pieces of paper. While this was going on, Sue positioned herself behind Alex and lightly placed her hands on his shoulders. As soon as she did this, he felt a tingling shoot through his body. It wasn't unlike the energies he'd felt when he was in his beloved woods or on top of his favorite mountain. It was an energy that spoke of calmness and nurturing—a balm to soothe his confused soul.

This isn't so bad. Maybe this blessing is what I've been looking for.

His relief that he'd found the right place was shattered when Brenda stood in front of him. She opened her mouth, but instead of reciting a gentle, lulling prayer, she began to bark at him.

"Repent, you worthless sinner. You're here to be blessed. You must let go of all those parts of yourself that do not serve you. You are a lost soul who must relinquish your ego so that you may come fully into who you really are."

Alex was shocked. He shrank within himself in an effort to escape Brenda's verbal assault. But it continued. More words of sin and unworthiness spewed from her. Guilt, remorse, and the certainty that he was an awful person went deeper, accompanied by the energy Sue was pouring into him. He was starting to believe these words as they imprinted themselves into his mind. He began to lose himself in this volley of insults and deliberate tearing down of his humanity. Just as he felt himself becoming completely swamped, he found the courage to swim up and out of this dark morass. He jumped out of the chair and confronted the two women.

"What the hell are you doing?" he demanded.

Confused by his reaction, Brenda hesitantly replied, "We're doing a blessing, Alex."

"I'm not feeling exactly blessed right now."

"That's because you interrupted. Blessings are about realizing what's wrong with you and letting it all go. Sue is filling you with holy prayer essence in order for you to purge all those bad aspects of yourself."

"I need to think about this," he mumbled as he turned and left the room. As he walked up the aisle, he felt their words and recriminations stuck to him like glue. He felt disoriented, as if he had no choice but to believe every one of their insults. In need of a familiar face, he sought out Angela.

"Are you okay?" Angela said as he came up to her.

"No. I feel weird."

"Here, sit down for a minute." He sat down in the last pew, and she ran to get him a glass of water. As he drank it, a tall man in a white robe approached him. He had dark-blonde hair and appeared to be in his late thirties.

"How are you doing, my son? I'm Père Peter. I heard you had a difficult time with the blessing."

"I guess."

Père Peter sat down next to him. "You didn't let the blessing finish."

"I feel worse than I've ever felt before. Was that supposed to happen?"

"You have to be torn down in order to build anew. However, you do seem to be more sensitive than most." He leaned over and placed his hand over Alex's. "We're about to start our service. Why don't you stay at least for that? It will be all right. I promise."

What Alex really wanted to do was leave. His energy felt completely off. But Angela squeezed his arm. "Let's give the service a chance," she whispered. "Look around. Everyone looks so happy."

Alex hesitated. Then nodded.

"Excellent!" Père Peter exclaimed as he clapped his hands together. He stood up and strode down the center aisle, his white robes flapping behind him.

Brenda and Sue were standing at either side of the podium. They each held a manila envelope, which they ripped open as Père Peter approached. As the man took his place at the podium, they withdrew the two white pieces of paper from each envelope.

"We are here in the name of salvation," Père Peter intoned. To Alex's surprise, the congregation repeated what he said, word for word. "We are here in the name of spiritual freedom." Again, the congregation repeated his words.

As if following a script, whatever Père Peter said, the group repeated. Alex watched the interchange, the almost mindless rote of repeating the minister's words verbatim. The energy grew in the room. It didn't take Alex long to recognize that the energy belonged exclusively to Père Peter. It was as if the repetition of his words from the congregation fed his own energy, which in turn was growing in leaps and bounds, taking over the room in its power.

To his amazement, Alex saw streams of dingy colors projecting out from the congregation. He watched as Père Peter's ego and energy consumed these colors, making it submissive to his will. He frowned. He didn't like what he was seeing and feeling.

In that moment, Alex understood just how sensitive he was to the energy of powerful people. How easy it was to surrender himself to the directed energy that was growing in the room. How quickly he could resemble the robot-like people seated all around him, giving away who they were to the man at the podium. It resembled what he'd felt at the

Moon and the Stars. This, however, was more intense. More purposeful. He glanced over to Angela and noticed she was getting caught up in it all. He tugged at her sleeve.

"We've got to leave," he whispered.

She looked at him as though she'd come out of a trance. "Uh . . . um . . ."

"Let's go, Angela. *Now*."

He grabbed her hand and pulled her out of the pew and through the back door. Outside, they jumped in his car and quickly drove away. It wasn't until they were some distance away from the church that she looked at him.

"What just happened back there?" she asked.

"I think I just learned something very important. Père Peter had everyone connect their energy to him. In turn, he was able to overpower them all with his own energy. It's scary to think what he could make them do if he wanted to."

"You mean like some kind of cult?"

"Yeah. It's frightening how energy can affect other people, especially energy coming from a very strong person."

"Like that Jim Jones guy? Or David Koresh, or a host of other people with strong, charismatic energy?" She shook her head to herself. "What are we going to do?"

"We don't have to do anything," he responded. "All I know is that I'm not going back there. That blessing really messed me up. I feel shaky inside and can't let go of these thoughts that I'm a terrible person."

"But you did get an answer by going there tonight. Look what you just figured out. Maybe there's more for you to discover."

He shook his head. "No. I think it's just a piece of a bigger puzzle. However, the first thing I need to do is get this bad feeling out of me. It's as if I have someone else's thoughts in my body and in my mind."

"How are you going to do that?"

"Tomorrow morning I'm going to hike the mountain."

The **Power** of Some

Many strong, powerful people in this world claim to have all the answers and the reasons behind everything. However, to sustain their strong sense of themselves, they gather others around them who are desperately seeking answers. Empaths quest more than most because their experiences don't have a frame of reference according to the rest of the world's thought process. This makes the empath vulnerable. But it also provides a valuable lesson. Empaths learn by energetic experiences.

In the story above, it was a bad experience for Alex, but it was also a very valuable experience. He learned firsthand how powerful people can manipulate the energy of others to sustain and magnify their own energy. This is what we call a dark teaching. You don't generally find these teachings in a book. You need to experience them for yourself. And you will know when you do experience it. It's frightening and disconcerting. Yet, at the same time, they are immensely valuable to your development as an empath.

How many times in our relationships are we told that we are imagining things, and that we are crazy, twisted, or led to believe we are the one with the problem? All along, our empathic ability is giving us red flags—energetic warnings—that something is amiss. Most times we shrug them off in our need not to rock the boat. Or in a deeper hope that our concerns are not real.

People around us use our insecurities or vulnerabilities as doorways into our energetic psyche. This is an attempt to break us down and feed from our desire to understand at a deeper level who we are. Narcissists manipulate truth to make it appear as if it's your fault. Cults use your need to belong to prey on your vulnerabilities. Others exert their strong personalities to make you doubt what you feel or think. They convince you that they are right and you are wrong. These are all people who use dark tools to overpower you energetically in an attempt to fill their own needs.

The Task Masters

8

Alex was angry over what had happened at the Angelic Church of Mysticism. Once again, he felt as though he'd been influenced in a way that made him lose who he was. They believed they were right, but he felt they were only taking advantage of others, as well as allowing themselves to be blindly taken advantage of through their ritual of the blessings. Words were given some kind of emotional life, and that life was put into him through Sue's hands to the point of overshadowing him with their self-righteousness. It was an energetic reprogramming in a way. They'd corrupted the word "blessing" by making it sound like something wonderful. Instead, the vulnerable persons were broken down by insults and guilt and whatever it took to break their will. Once their will was wavering, Père Peter swooped in and cemented his control by swamping the person's weak energetic will with his own immensely strong energetic will. In the process, he became their savior.

Alex shuddered at what he perceived to be their malicious intent. What he couldn't understand was why he seemed to be the only one who'd caught on to what they were doing. Angela thought he was overreacting. That hurt him.

Maybe it was because she hadn't gone through the blessing. Maybe he was more sensitive, as Père Peter had said. As much as he hated to admit it, he still felt the barbs of Brenda's words stuck in his psyche, making him feel worse about himself.

The more he thought about what she'd said, the lower he felt. Part of him knew it was ridiculous to feel the way he did. He didn't consider himself an unrepentant sinner or a lost soul. Yet, a small part of him wondered if he was indeed guilty of treating people badly, of turning his back on those who needed his help. He thought about the times he'd lost his temper with his mother and siblings, of the situations where he'd fought with his father. The awful words he'd said.

Maybe I am a lost soul, after all.

Finally, he turned off the light and crept into bed, hoping the hike in the morning would help him regain his sense of self. And ease the guilt in his heart.

He was just drifting off to sleep when he heard a voice whisper in his ear, "Do you want to know the truth? We are the truth. We're now here with you."

Alex opened his eyes and looked around the bedroom. There was nothing there; just his clothes thrown over the dresser and his school books on the floor. Thinking the voice had come to him in a dream, he started to lie back down. Tomorrow was going to be a busy day, and he needed his sleep. Settling down, the hairs suddenly stood up on the back of his neck. He looked to his right and to his left. There was nothing there.

But he hadn't looked up.

He didn't want to. He inwardly fought against looking up. But he had no choice. The prickling on his skin told him something was above him. He had to look up. He had to see, if only to know what to protect himself against.

Holding his breath, Alex rolled his eyes upward. And swallowed the scream.

There was a black shadow hovering above the bed, inches from the top of his head. It looked like a wraith, with its ragged black robes suspended over his prone body on the bed.

Alex tried to jump out of bed. To his horror, he realized he couldn't move. He was paralyzed. Helpless. At the mercy of whatever this thing was.

He opened his mouth to yell for help, but nothing came out. His words were as paralyzed as his body. An inner terror overcame him. He watched helplessly as the wraith drew closer to him. To his face. To his mouth. Draining his energy. His very essence.

Dear God. It's going to suck away my soul. Help me! Someone please help me!

Alex abruptly sat up in bed, his heart pounding, his palms sweaty. He rubbed his eyes and looked up at the ceiling. There was nothing there. But it didn't stop him from scrambling out of bed and dashing out of the bedroom.

When he reached the living room, he collapsed on the couch. His stomach and chest were so tight that he wanted to throw up. He took deep gulps of air to stave off the nausea.

What the hell was that thing? Was it real? Had he only dreamed it? Or had it really been there? Paralyzing him? Robbing him of his energy?

It took him a long while to calm down. Once he felt back in control of his emotions, he tried to figure out what had just happened. Was it the church? Was it Germaine?

Had the shadow appeared because he'd gone to bed in such a low state? Because he'd believed the words Brenda flung at him? Because, since experiencing the blessing, he hadn't liked himself very much?

A light bulb went off in his head. If it was true that the shadow appeared because he'd been in such a vulnerable state, would it stay away if he changed his way of thinking? If he chose not to believe Brenda's words? If he chose not to plug into negative situations he saw all around him? Could it be that his experiences both with Germaine and Père Peter were meant to happen to teach him how energy works? In order for him to gain more confidence in his wielding of his own energetic experience?

As the realization of these words sunk in, he felt his energy change. Tension oozed out of him and his stomach unclenched.

In a more relaxed state now, he lay on the couch and drifted off to sleep. Once again, he was confronted with the dark shadow.

"I can't be afraid. I won't be afraid."

He continued to focus on those words and to focus on the fact that he was stronger than he thought. He'd had the courage to leave both Germaine and the church. He hadn't blindly stayed. He'd known enough to walk out the door.

He knew he had to do the same thing here. He needed to leave the fear behind.

But it wasn't quite working. The dark shadow was making him feel like he did whenever he felt marginalized, whenever he felt like a loser, or just one more face in a sea of faces. As if the shadow had an energy of its own that Alex was reacting to. He began to feel that familiar sense of despair.

He desperately tried to find a way to get this thing to back off. A vague memory came up from his time with the psychiatrist. Dr. Taylor had talked about creating a happy place in his mind to help him focus, especially in times of fear. Desperate, he knew he needed to do something to make this thing go away.

There was only one place he could think of that truly was his happy place. It was the top of the mountain where he hiked whenever he was feeling blue.

He conjured up a picture of the mountain in his mind's eye. He felt the breeze on his face and the sun on his back as he sat on the large, flat rock atop the mountain and looked down at the valley below. His focus shifted from the black shadow to the peace he felt there. Slowly, he began to feel better. Yet, if he took his focus off the mountain and back on the wraith, it was in his face, chuckling at his misery.

He spent the next few minutes ping-ponging back and forth between the mountain, where his energy felt good, and the shadow, where his energy felt constricted.

He couldn't keep it up much longer. The effort was exhausting him. With one final push, he focused everything he had on the mountain.

It was the alarm that woke him up. He sat up on the couch and looked around. It was light out. And he'd survived.

Focus

As an empath, you may have energies that are very dark and very physically debilitating presenting themselves to you. We would be lying if we denied that there are things that go bump in the night. Not all of them are pleasant. Is it possible they serve a purpose in helping you learn to stand in your power? If you go into fear, you feed these energies. You come out of it drained and feeling awful, as if you'd been manipulated by a bully. One method to get out of the fear is to focus on something else. Religions over the millennia have used rosary beads, mala beads, and prayers in order to focus the mind. These days, you can use a crystal or a recited prayer or create a happy place where you can redirect your energy and find solace. These all keep your attention focused. If you don't pay the darkness any mind, you're not feeding it your energy. However, sometimes the darkness will escalate in order to get your attention. As we always say, you must be doing something right if these energies find you enough of a threat to frighten you so that you shut yourself away or deny your own power and abilities.

Frightful
Creatures

As Alex pushed himself off the couch, he felt drained and very heavy, as though he'd run a marathon or after he'd experienced an emotional upheaval. Knowing that the dark wraith had fed on his own feelings of inadequacy, he made the decision not to go there. He needed to dispel those feelings Brenda had evoked in him. As he focused on the mountain and the hike he planned to take after class, he felt his energy lifting. The darkness wasn't completely gone, but it had detached enough that he could go about his day.

Getting into his car, his mind drifted to Angela. It was still hard to believe that she'd actually asked him to go to that church with her. The church itself may have been a dud, but he felt a connection with her. He hoped that she felt the same way.

To his delight, he ran into her once again in the cafeteria.

"How are you doing, Alex?" she greeted as they sat down at a table together. "Did you get any sleep?"

He wasn't about to share his dream about the creepy shadow. Instead, he answered, "Off and on. It wasn't a restful sleep."

She nodded. "Yeah, mine wasn't either. I know I had some weird dreams because I woke up in a cold sweat. But for the life of me, I can't remember them."

Lucky you.

"When I finally crawled out of bed this morning, I felt as though I'd been hit by a Mac truck." She sighed. "I hate when I feel so low. It takes me forever to get out of the funk."

"Come to the mountain with me," Alex blurted out. When she looked at him, he blushed. "What I mean is . . . well . . . there's this mountain I hike that always lifts my spirits, especially when I'm sitting at the top. I'm heading there after class today. Why don't you come with me? The sunset alone may help with your blues."

She studied him for a long moment. Just as he was convinced she'd turn him down or, worse, laugh in his face, she smiled. "Sounds like a plan."

His mood soared as they arranged to meet up later that afternoon.

As they finished lunch and went their separate ways, Alex was amazed to discover how much better he felt. His heaviness was still there, but it wasn't as draining. Nor as debilitating. During his afternoon classes, he concentrated more on Angela than he did on what the teacher was saying. Suddenly, in the middle of his daydreams, a thought squirmed its way in that made him sit back in his chair with a thud.

What if Angela was just stringing him along? What if she really thought he was a loser and was with him only to amuse herself? What if he was what he'd always suspected—a big, lousy, stinking freak? Let's face it. She was a beautiful woman. Why would she waste her time and attention on someone like him? The thoughts took on a life of their own and spiraled, taking his mood down with them.

His energy immediately plummeted. As he felt himself starting to slide into despondency, he suddenly caught a movement out of the corner of his eye. He caught his breath. He couldn't be certain, but he could swear he'd just seen a glimpse of that damned wraith.

He frowned. What the hell? This can't be real.

Packing up his books, he stepped out into the hallway. Through the crowd of students, he saw Angela. She raised her hand and gave him a wide grin and a wave before she melted back into the crush. Her smile and wave banished the dark thoughts from his mind. Once again he felt his energy soar. Walking to his next class, he noticed there weren't any shadows in his periphery. He pondered this and had what he would later describe as an "a-ha" moment. It seemed that when his mood dipped, the shadows appeared. But when his mood was happy, they were nowhere to be found.

Was there a connection?

A few hours later found the two slowly making their way up the mountain. With each step, he felt any tension or any doubt ooze out of him. They chitchatted as they walked. Angela shared her experiences growing up, feeling other people's emotions, and not knowing why or what to do about them. Alex listened. Occasionally he offered a word or a comment, but his shy nature precluded him from sharing what he'd been through. Maybe it was because he still grappled with the need to be normal, even in the face of what he'd experienced. It was better to keep the wraith and his own feelings of inadequacy hidden. He didn't want to scare Angela by appearing to be the freak he secretly feared he was. Her stories were similar to what he'd been through, but they came nowhere near to many of the things he'd faced.

They reached the top and sat quietly side by side watching the sun dip down over the horizon.

"This is fantastic," Angela sighed. "Thank you for bringing me up here. I feel so much better already. This really is an awesome place."

"I'm glad you wanted to come. This is where I go when I need to unwind. It's as if the mountain drains the heaviness out of me."

"Is that the tingling I feel in my feet?" He nodded. "Wow. That's amazing."

They watched the reds and oranges swirl throughout the sky before Alex stood up. "We'd better head down before it gets too dark."

He helped her down the more difficult parts, savoring the feel of her hand in his. He longed to keep her hand clasped in his, but he didn't have the courage. Instead, he felt a slight ache in his heart each time she withdrew her hand from his.

They made it down in record time—too fast for Alex. He enjoyed Angela's company and wanted to relish it for as long as he could. Before he knew it, they were back in the parking lot. He drove her back to her dorm, all the while hoping she would invite him upstairs or suggest they go grab a bite to eat. The hike had given him an appetite. Instead, as soon as he pulled up to the dorm, she hopped out.

"That was great, Alex. Thanks for taking me up there. It was so worth it. I've got a ton of homework to do, so I'll say good night." Just as she was about to slam the door, her cell phone rang. She whipped it out of her pocket and answered it. "Hey Brad, how are you? It's been ages since I've heard from you! Of course I'd love to have dinner with you tonight. Where do you want to go?"

She turned and left, happily speaking to Brad. And left the passenger door open.

Alex's euphoria instantly evaporated as he climbed out of the car and slowly closed the passenger door. As he slid back into his seat and drove away, he felt that heaviness descend over him like a wet, rainy cloud. Damn it, he really was a loser. No wonder Angela wanted to get away from him as quickly as possible. She had no time to have dinner with him. But she did for this Brad, whoever he was.

The more Alex thought about it, the more his energy slid down the precipice until he was right back where he'd been the night before. This time, however, the heaviness hadn't been caused by a church, or by a Brenda or a Germaine. It had been caused by his own judgment of himself.

He was right on the edge. Just one step and he'd topple over into a swamp of deep depression. Recognizing that, he pulled back and tried to focus on the mountain. His energy ratcheted up a little bit. But it was close.

Driving through the streets toward his apartment, he felt as though he were being stalked. He glanced into his rearview mirror into the back seat, expecting to see the black shadow. It wasn't there, but he felt *something* around him pulling him down. He had images of Angela thrown into his face, his grip on his energy slipping.

By the time he arrived home, all he wanted to do was flop onto his bed. Lying there, he stared up at the ceiling, determined to focus on his happy place. At the same time, he felt his stomach getting tighter and tighter. Suddenly he felt a shift of energy so strong that he looked up. And saw the figure of a man beginning to manifest at the foot of his bed.

He scrambled up against the headboard in terror as the figure came into focus.

Dear God, it has no eyes.

Black sockets stared back at him.

I'm going crazy, he thought frantically to himself. *What's going on? Shadows, bad thoughts, nightmares. Now this.*

He lost his focus and the fear took over. The battle began.

Thoughts, feelings, emotions, and visions all crashed into some kind of energetic horror show. They all seemed to be coming from the man with no eyes.

He realized in horror that this was a battle for his very soul. The only weapon he had was to focus. Somehow. Someway.

He forced himself to conjure up the mountain. However, the happy place was working less and less.

He felt a dense energy seeping into his body. His mind filled with terrifying thoughts that he was about to die. Because he wasn't worthy to live. Whatever this creature was, it was determined to take his humanity.

He opened up his mouth to scream, but nothing came out. Instead, all he could do was moan.

This is not real. It can't be real. But it is real.

What happened at the church came back to him. Brenda's words, the dingy energy, all swirling together to create a reaction from him, causing him to sink deeper into fear and negativity.

Somehow, through the fear and terror, he wondered if what he was feeling was being projected at him from the man with no eyes. Was it possible that his energy was being deliberately decreased, making him more vulnerable? Or was he *allowing* his energy to be decreased?

His moaning awoke him.

He jumped out of bed and began to pace. What had triggered such a horrible nightmare? It had felt so real. Was it because of his reaction to Angela's phone call with Brad? Was it a repeat of what had happened the night before with the wraith?

Once he'd starting thinking about what a loser he was, and how stupid he'd been to ever believe Angela would want to be with him, his energy had tanked. And he'd had the nightmare.

He slowed his pacing as it occurred to him that he was allowing himself to become vulnerable according to how he was feeling. When he was in a good space, he didn't have these nightmares. But when he went into that dark place . . .

He sat down on the edge of the bed as a realization hit him.

It's when I allow myself to become vulnerable that I'm attacked.

But there was more than vulnerability going on here. Did the projection from the man with no eyes create the vulnerability? And had he unwittingly stepped into it?

The **In-Between** Space

As an empath, you probably spend much of your time trying to be in a space of feeling good, feeling safe. Countless times these spaces are found when you hide yourself away from people, or keep to yourself because interaction with others makes you feel uncomfortable. The reality is that you have to be part of life. You can't hide away forever. Because you deal with the highs and lows of energy, these are lessons to be learned between these two spectrums. Once you touch the top of the mountain, that's where you want to stay because that's the place you feel your best. You feel safe. You feel good. You feel accepted. However, when you touch the depths of the valley, you know you don't want to stay there because that's where your fears, your insecurities, and your uncomfortability reside. What about the in-between space? How do you function there? Because it's within the in-between space that things take advantage and try to keep you from reaching that higher energy.

It is so easy to get us to react when things don't go our way. Unrequited love, the job you didn't get, etc. Instantly, you react from this emotional situation. Those who are at their weakest react the deepest. As an empath, with your energetic sensitivity, your lows and highs are even more pronounced. You have a stronger energy source, and in that, you are more able to create these highs and lows. Herein lies the vulnerability. A projection of an energy that is aligned with one of your fears can very quickly make you believe and sense the intention of whatever is projected at you. The intention is to break you down, to make you prey in order to feed off the fear you leak. In this space, simply being positive with words or visualization doesn't always bring you back to peace. It is because of your sensitivity to energy that intentions of lesser vibrations quickly make you retreat back to old learned behaviors. As it is with words, you can give them meaning. In that meaning, a dualistic label of good or bad becomes what you decide.

It's also the same with your energetic perceptions. Vibrations can take on the role of good or bad, pleasant or unpleasant. What if they are just what they are? Just an energy—just a vibration. It allows you to take back your judgment of the experience, just like the words that you give meanings to. If you just allow yourself to be present, you will learn that these judged experiences have no way to affect you. Responding opens a doorway that begins the draining of your energy. Remember, the predator will soon disappear when there is nothing to feed on.

The Art
of Protection

10

When Alex awoke the next morning, he was beyond tired. Yet, at the same time, he was having some important realizations.

He knew he had some kind of ability. Others around him could easily affect how he felt, but he now knew he had the ability to change his energetic experience by changing his thought process. Last night he'd learned how easily he could screw himself up if something didn't go the way he wanted. His despair over Angela going to dinner with Brad seemed to put a bull's-eye on his back. And something last night took a shot right through that bull's-eye.

So how to deal with this? How to live a normal life? Was he always going to have to patrol his emotions, constantly looking over his shoulder to make sure the darkness didn't attack him? Was he really going to have to watch every thought? As it was, the mere thought of going to sleep terrified him.

There had to be an answer somewhere.

At the end of his World Religions class that morning, he waited until all the students were gone before he approached his teacher. "Mr. Myers, I really love this class. It's taught me a lot. Recently though, I've been wondering if there are any religions that got into the subject of dreams?"

The short, bespectacled man slowly put his class notes into his briefcase. "There are many older religions that understood the significance of dreams. Some used them as healing tools; others, as a way to divine with the gods. Still others saw them as something to be avoided because they believed darker entities lived in what they called the in-between space—that space that lies between the time we are awake and the time when we fall asleep."

Alex remembered the dark shadow and the man with no eyes and inwardly shuddered.

Mr. Myers placed his hand on the young man's shoulder. "I've spent years studying these older religions. And I can tell you, we don't always have to see things to know they exist."

"Thank you, Mr. Myers."

As he started to turn away, the teacher added, "Be careful in your quest, Alex. Sometimes when you open the door, you'll find it's not so easy to shut it."

Alex walked away with an uneasy feeling, yet he was curious at the same time. He knew he had to do something. He wasn't about to spend his life dealing with the man with no eyes or the dark shadow disturbing his dreams.

After class that day, he went to the library, stumbling onto a section dedicated to the occult. He began to thumb through several books. It wasn't until he picked up a book called *The Art of Protection* that he felt he was onto something.

He checked it out, and as soon as he got home he began to read. The first chapter had to do with stones used to ward off the evil eye, a belief that someone could curse another through a malevolent stare. He quickly started taking notes.

Cultures used different techniques to ward off evil—prayers, incantations, salt, charms, herbs, incense, and other articles. As he took in all this information, he wondered where he could get his hands on some of the items mentioned. Germaine's store instantly came to mind. At first he was reluctant to return there—he hadn't forgotten how much the man had manipulated him. However, he felt more empowered now. And it was the only place in town where he could purchase what he needed.

You're just going to have to suck it up if you want to survive.

Walking into the store, he was drawn to a display of smoky quartz. According to the book he'd read the night before, this was an excellent protection stone. He picked one up and felt a tingle in his palm as the energy seemed to move through him. He instantly felt lighter.

"So you decided to come back?"

He turned to find Germaine at his elbow.

"Just wanted to pick up a few things, that's all."

Germaine looked at the stone in his hand and gave a small, knowing smile. "Of course," he said. "Feel free to browse."

Alex forced himself to ignore the man and his annoying smugness. He walked around, amazed that he'd never noticed the books and New Age paraphernalia when he'd been there before.

He picked up some incense, some protection salt, and the smoky quartz. He brought them up to the register. "Is there anything else you want?" Germaine asked.

"This should do it for now."

"Suit yourself." He rang up the sale and handed the bag to Alex. "Good luck protecting yourself."

Alex jerked his head up and stared at Germaine. The man met his eye, that irritating smile playing at the edge of his mouth.

Determined not to allow himself to be cowed by this man again, Alex put the cash down on the counter, grabbed the bag, and left the store. He felt Germaine's eyes boring into his back, but he refused to give into it. He was protected now. Nothing was going to torment him again.

On his way home, he decided to stop off and get a coffee. Entering the coffee shop, he was standing in line when he felt a tap on his shoulder. Turning, he saw it was Angela.

"Hey, Alex. How are you doing?"

His energy was all over the place. He was happy to see her, while he was still hurt over her phone call with Brad. "Okay," he answered.

"You ever recover from that crazy church we went to?"

He shrugged. "Sometimes I let people's moods affect me too much."

"Ah, don't worry about it. I do the same thing."

They ordered their cups of coffee. He was about to leave when she pointed to a corner. "Why don't we sit down? That is, if you don't have to dash off somewhere."

Alex knew he should just leave. What was the point of letting her hurt him again? But he couldn't. He liked her. A lot. And he still held out hope that if they spent enough time together, she'd start to view him as someone she'd like to date.

Sitting down, Angela once again shared her experiences of being affected by other people's energies. "I especially hate it when people aren't being authentic," she said as she took a sip of her coffee.

"What do you mean by that?"

"Oh you know. When someone says something that you just *know* isn't the truth. It's hard to explain, but it's like a feeling comes over me that tells me they are full of it. Haven't you ever felt that way?"

Alex nodded. "Quite often, actually."

"It's weird, but helpful at the same time." Angela looked at her watch and stood up. "I'd better get going. I'm meeting my mom for dinner. Let's make plans to get together again. It's always interesting talking to you."

Well, that wasn't so bad. It hadn't lasted as long as he would have wanted, but at least she'd admitted she liked talking to him. It was a start.

Standing up from the table, Alex realized he wasn't ready to go home just yet. He didn't want to admit it, but he was nervous that the wraith or the man with no eyes would be waiting for him. It was then that he remembered the articles he'd bought. He picked up the bag and weighed it in his hand.

Well, tonight's as good a night as any to find out if this stuff I bought really works.

He carefully placed the items on his nightstand. He then lay down on the bed. And waited. He felt his eyelids closing, but he was frightened to fall asleep. To be on the safe side, he grabbed the smoky quartz and shoved it under his pillow. He instantly felt better. Enough that he closed his eyes and allowed sleep to overtake him.

"Alex."

His eyes shot open. He turned his head back and forth, still feeling the breath in his ear where his name had been whispered. He shoved his hand under the pillow and grabbed onto the smoky quartz. Once again, he felt a sense of calm come over him as the energy of his fear ground out of his feet. He closed his eyes again and felt sleep beginning to overtake him.

"Alex."

The voice was louder this time. He abruptly sat up and caught his breath. Surrounding his bed were figures dressed in old-fashioned clothing. He couldn't tell who they were. He couldn't tell *what* they were. None of the figures had faces, but he was determined not to give into his anxiety. Not this time. He gripped the smoky quartz tightly in his hand.

"You are not real," he shouted at the figures. "You are not real, and you are not going to frighten me."

To his surprise, he felt his fear dissolve. As it did, so did the figures. He looked down at the smoky quartz in his hand and whistled. "Holy crap. It works!"

Feeling **Safe**

In the search to feel safe, empaths find themselves attached to items they believe will keep them safe. There are many purported spiritual items such as crystals, incense, and salts that have an energetic vibration of their own. This energetic vibration tends to be removed from the typical experiences of fear and negativity, as if they serve as purifiers of that lower vibrational energy. When you use these items as a personal energetic tool, their vibration reminds you of what you are missing energetically within yourself or are capable of obtaining through a higher vibrational experience. Much like teachers, they serve to help you remember. But what happens when the teacher isn't there? Or the teacher becomes the crutch? How will you survive those moments if you no longer have the crystal, the salt, or the teacher? These items can serve as a reminder of what you're capable of— being in a space of no fear. Because truthfully, you are more powerful than any energetic intrusion from a negative source. Just as stones and crystals project a life of no fear, this is their teaching to you. The best protection will always be no fear. No fear allows no leakage of your energy. No leakage of your energy allows nothing to feed off you.

The Broken Heart

11

When Alex awoke the next morning, he was still holding on to the smoky quartz. He looked down at it, amazed at the power it held. It had actually saved him from whatever had surrounded his bed the night before. After they disappeared, he was able to fall back into a deep sleep; in fact, the best sleep he'd had in weeks.

As he showered and prepared for school, he found himself filled with confidence. And a deep sense of hope that he'd finally found a huge part of the puzzle of what was happening to him. It was a strange sensation for him. He'd never felt so courageous or confident before: it was as though he could take on the world and win. He couldn't wait to share with Angela, not only about how much the crystal had helped, but about everything in his life.

Just before reaching his first class, he took out his cell and gave Angela a call, asking her to meet him at the coffee shop later that afternoon.

Throughout the rest of the day, Alex felt like a different person. He felt lighter. Happier. His newly found confidence, and the crystal he kept safely tucked in his jeans pocket, gave him a sense of peace that had been lacking in his life for so long.

He couldn't wait to see Angela and tell her all about it.

The hours dragged on interminably. He rehearsed in his mind just how he'd tell Angela all he wanted to tell her. She was sensitive herself. She was the perfect person to understand all the crazy experiences he'd been through. There was a connection between them that he couldn't deny. He wanted to be with her, to be a part of her life. In fact, the last thing she'd said to him when they'd met at the café was how much she liked talking to him. If he played his cards right, they'd be spending a lot more time talking. And climbing his favorite mountain. And doing all the things that couples who were falling in love did.

Finally, his last class was over. He literally flew across campus and burst into the coffee shop. He scanned the tables, and his heart leapt with joy when he saw her sitting in the back. She was reading a book, and he took a moment to study the curve of her cheek and the way her blonde hair curled along her shoulders. His heart was so full of feeling for her that he felt as though he could float across the room.

He slid into the chair opposite her and wanted to take her hands. But he didn't dare. Not yet. Not until he spoke with her and told her everything that was in his heart. Instead, he smiled. She looked up and met his eye.

"You look like the cat that swallowed the canary," she teased.

He laughed. "Maybe I did." When she gave him a quizzical look, he added, "I'm glad you're here. I wanted to explain to you why I sometimes come off like I'm tense or out of sorts. Or why I reacted the way I did back at the church. I know you'll understand because you're sensitive. Just like I am. In fact, you and I are very much alike."

With the courage and confidence he'd been feeling all day, he told her about his life. About what others would consider his over-the-top experiences. He shared what happened when he tried to say the prayer for the dead deer. He tried to describe the incredible energy he'd felt when the spirit of the deer not only appeared to him but had actually walked into him. He told her about the bullies he'd had to put up with in high school, and what he'd discovered about their need to take his energy to make themselves feel better. Lastly, he told her about the wraith, the man with no eyes, and how the crystal had saved him from the figures with no faces. When he was done, he felt as though he'd been talking for hours. Yet he felt wonderful. For the first time in his life, he felt unburdened by all he'd been carrying inside. Sitting there with Angela, telling her about his life, he was no longer the freak or the loner. He wasn't the terrible person Brenda had tried to make him believe he was. He was simply a man who, for whatever reason, was extremely sensitive to energy. Who had experiences that were trying to teach him about himself. More importantly, he'd finally found something that made him feel safe. And with that safety came trust. Not only of himself, but in her as well. Because he'd finally found someone who was just like him.

He grinned at her. "So you see, there was a reason why I acted the way I did. I was so confused and scared. I didn't know which way to turn. But that crystal last night really helped. It made me see that these energies I feel can be controlled. I don't have to be a victim anymore."

"You mean that smoky quartz you bought at that weirdo's place?" Angela asked.

"Yeah. It's totally amazing."

He was so caught up in the emotions of feeling safe and feeling something for this woman that he finally gave in to what he'd been wanting to do since they'd first gotten together. He reached out and took her hands in his. "I can't tell you how awesome it is to meet someone who understands all of this. I couldn't have made it this far without your help. I want you to feel as safe and protected as I do. We'll go to the Moon and the Stars right now and get you a smoky quartz. I'll even pay for it. It will help you as much as it's helped me."

Alex was unprepared for what happened next. As he watched her with a goofy smile on his face, Angela gently slipped her hands out of his grasp and placed them in her lap. She looked at her coffee cup and at the book that was still open in front of her. She looked at everything. Except Alex. "You don't need to do that," she replied quietly.

His smile slid off his face as he felt her energy completely withdraw from him. His heart, which had been flying on cloud nine just two seconds before, now plummeted down to earth, where it crashed and burned into a thousand pieces.

"I—I'm sorry," he mumbled through the pain that was bubbling up in his chest. "I didn't mean to offend you."

"You didn't."

"I just wanted you to understand . . . to know that we're both sensitive and—"

"We're not," she swiftly interrupted. "That is, we're not alike, Alex. I know you think we are, but I haven't had any of the experiences you just described. Yeah, I feel other people's emotions, but I've never had a deer walk through me. And I've certainly never had people without faces or black shadows attack me in my bedroom at night. That's intense. Way too intense for me." She grabbed her book and dropped it into her bag. She then stood up. "You're a nice guy, Alex. Really, you are. But I'm not looking for a relationship right now. And I'm definitely not looking to have monsters, or whatever you described, popping up in my dreams or at the foot of my bed any time soon. I'm sorry."

She swept past him and out of the café. Alex sat there, his entire world lying in pieces around him. He could barely breathe as a sharp pain tore through his heart. As if she'd not only stabbed him in the heart with her words but literally sliced him open with a knife. Now he knew what the singers meant when they sang about a broken heart. He felt as though his own heart had shattered.

He blinked back the tears that stung his eyes. And felt completely stupid. He was usually so good at picking up energy, but this one had blindsided him. He'd opened himself up only to be shut down. Tossed aside as though he were an inconvenience.

No, as though he were a freak.

It was too much.

With his head bowed, he hurried out of the café and spent the next hour aimlessly driving around. By the time he returned to his apartment, he'd shut down emotionally. Unable to bear the anguish of what he was feeling, he made sure not to feel anything at all.

He took out the smoky quartz and held it in his hand. It had protected him against the darkness in his room. He could only hope it would now protect him from the darkness within his own soul.

The Feelings of Love

As an empath, you come into this world with your heart wide open, expecting to have a lifetime filled with love. As you go through this life, you spend a great deal of time trying to find love, be in love, give love, and, yes, be validated as loving, or worthy of being loved. Many empaths seem to find themselves in challenging childhoods where the experience of love isn't exactly a Hallmark greeting card filled with rainbows, unicorns, and poems declaring how wonderfully full of love all existence is. Maybe by some divine dictate, it has been decided that as an empath, you've come to this world to experience what love *isn't*. No matter the case, there is one thing for certain. You are destined to have a lifetime filled with the lessons of love.

Love tends to be dictated by an energy you can't help but feel, which in turn creates all kinds of confusion. The examples below illustrate this:

PARTNER: I love you.

EMPATH: I'm not feeling it.

PARTNER: Look what I do for you. That proves I love you.

EMPATH: Hmmmm. I'm feeling you do what you do because you really want something else.

PARTNER: You're so cute. Let's go on a date.

EMPATH (thinking to themselves): You're cute, too. But for some reason, I feel like I want to throw up.

PARTNER: I was just out with my friends. Nothing happened.

EMPATH: You're hiding something. I just know you are.

These may sound comical, but your inner love barometer makes you question what it is you're feeling, seeing, hearing, and thinking, because something isn't adding up. And just what isn't adding up? Your experience of projected energy.

Many times you tend to hang on longer than you should because you're feeling such intense love; it creates confusion about what the reality of the relationship you're in truly is. Since love is a projected energy, and you're here to learn the lessons of what love truly is, who projects love better than an empath? No one. So guess what? Because of your strong need for love, what you are actually attracting is your most difficult lesson—someone who probably is unable to love, surrounded by walls created by their own personal wounds. So begins the class syllabus of your love life. The love that you need and desire so deeply, screaming see me, feel me, understand me, projects out from you. It hits the walls put up by your lover and, like a mirror, reflects back to you. All the while, you are confused because you think this intense love you're feeling is from the other person, when in fact it is your own love projected back to you.

What does this teach you? The most important realization in this classroom of love is you. Loving yourself, trusting yourself, learning yourself, and the most important lesson of all—the purpose of you. It doesn't seem fair that sometimes it takes a broken heart to realize what's important, but as you'll see, because you're an empath, nothing but real love will ever be enough. Anything less is your vulnerability on the dark road of love.

As the difficult lessons of love are learned and you begin to illuminate the love that you are, your loving vibration begins to increase. Neediness for love changes to being love. Love then becomes a choice, not a need.

The Edge of the Cliff

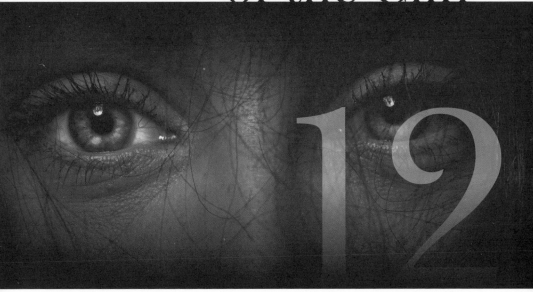

Alex didn't want to get out of bed. He didn't want to go to class. He didn't want to do anything. What he'd felt for Angela was a feeling so deep that he'd never experienced anything like it before. But she hadn't wanted it. Hadn't wanted him.

He didn't know what to do. He felt himself sliding into a deep depression. Maybe he really was unlovable. Maybe he was too much of a freak. Who the hell had men with no eyes appearing in their dreams?

As he sat on the couch feeling sorry for himself, he saw a dark shadow dart by out of the corner of his eye.

Great. Exactly what he needed.

He immediately tried to go to his happy place. He grabbed his smoky quartz and held it tightly in his hand. Nothing changed. If anything, the shadows intensified.

What was he missing? What was he doing wrong? The crystal had worked the night before. Why wasn't it working now? Had he sunk so low that nothing was going to save him?

Alex tried to rouse himself to climb out of the black hole he'd tumbled down into. But it hurt too much. Everything, including the shadows, seemed so pointless. The more he tried to grab onto some frame of reference, he became numb. All his senses void. Even his thoughts lacked the power to shift him above it all.

He felt that the darkness was winning. If he continued wallowing in his misery, it would soon be too late. As it had so many times in the past when all seemed lost, something switched inside him. He suddenly remembered all the dark emotional moments he'd been through in his life. There always seemed to be some kind of a choice he had to make. Up or down. Sink or swim. Eat or be eaten.

This was one of those moments.

I can't let these things win. I can't let Angela win. She rejected me and it hurts, but I can't let that destroy my life. I've survived this far. I'll survive again.

The shadows fell back as a resolve to get through this bubbled up within Alex. They retreated, but they didn't disappear. He knew they were waiting for his resolve to falter—just one small crack they could slither through. But he wasn't going to let that happen.

He recalled Germaine claiming he was a healer. Yet he wasn't so desperate that he'd return to that man for anything. Yet, Germaine couldn't be the only healer in town. There had to be someone out there who could help him.

He thumbed through his cell phone, looking for healers, and a website for a healing center called Earthsong caught his attention. They declared themselves to be holistic healers; seeing that the place wasn't too far from him, Alex gathered his courage and called.

"We've just had a cancellation," the receptionist told him when he asked for the soonest available appointment. "Can you be here in an hour?"

"Perfect. I'll be there," he said.

As soon as he hung up, he felt himself calming down. He was convinced the cancellation was a sign, telling him he was going in the right direction. That calmed him down even more. The darkness retreated further.

An hour later, Alex found himself standing in a reception area that was very soothing to the senses. Soft music played in the background as the sweet scent of patchouli permeated the air. It was a far cry from what he'd felt when he'd walked into the Angelic Church of Mysticism or Germaine's shop. There, he'd felt on edge. But here, he felt relaxed. And somehow comforted.

A middle-aged woman wearing a lavender-colored tunic over a pair of white slacks greeted him. She had her white hair pulled back into a twist, and her face lit up with a smile as she approached him.

"Hello, I'm Lena. You must be Alex." Her voice was gentle, and he immediately felt at ease with her. "Why don't you come back with me to my healing room?"

He followed her down a short corridor and into a room where a Reiki table was set up. There were small white candles lit, throwing off a dim yet peaceful light. Lena sat at a desk and indicated to Alex to sit down in the chair next to her desk.

"So Alex, why are you here today?"

Later, when he had time to think about it, he was surprised how his reticence disappeared, as if her soothing energy gave him an unspoken permission to bare his soul. Before he knew what he was doing, he shared his deep sense of loneliness experiencing all he'd experienced for so many years. When he was done, he looked at her.

"What's wrong with me? Am I crazy? Is it normal to see all that I do and feel all I do?"

Without hesitation, Lena replied, "First of all, you're not crazy. Second of all, there's nothing wrong with you. You're an empath, Alex. And that's what empaths do. They see and feel so many things on so many levels."

"I'm a what?"

"An empath. A human sponge that soaks up all the emotions and feelings of everyone and everything around you."

"Does being an empath include dealing with all these dark things I've been seeing lately?"

"Let me put it this way. Because empaths feel so much, they have a great deal of energy. When you're an emotional mess, do these dark entities show up more?"

"Yeah they do. Are they real?"

"Well, they were pretty real to you, weren't they?"

"Definitely."

"What did you do about it?"

"I thought I'd found some teachers who could help me make them go away."

"How did that work out for you?"

He guffawed. "Not very well. They ended up taking advantage of me."

"That can happen, especially to people who have been searching for so long for the answers to why they are the way they are. Your innocence and desire to learn made you vulnerable. Did those experiences teach you anything?"

"When it happened, I was angry and bitter. But I've come to realize that going through it all taught me the strength of myself."

"Including dealing with those dark entities in your room?"

"At first, I was terrified. There are so many beliefs about good and evil that it was hard to shift out of all of that. I tried to think them away by going to my happy place, but that didn't work for very long. I thought I was losing my mind when I started seeing these shadows at school. I felt as though they were stalking me."

"They were. So what did you do about it?"

He took out the smoky quartz from his pocket and showed it to her. "I bought this and it calmed me down. As I calmed down, they went away. I felt my body tingling, just like I feel when I hike my favorite mountain. I was so sure I'd found something that would keep me completely safe from them. However, they came back this morning when I realized how much of a fool I was for thinking that Angela would ever care for a freak like me. This time, they wouldn't go away."

She looked at his crystal then pointed to all the ones she had displayed in her healing room. "Do you see these crystals, Alex?" He nodded. "They're all teachers. They serve as reminders of the energy of you."

"I'm not sure I understand."

"When it comes to energy, I've found it's much better to have you feel what I'm saying rather than listening to me throw words at you. If you lie down on the healing table, I'll show you what I mean."

Alex hesitated. He'd already been made to feel the fool by Germaine, Père Peter, and Angela, and he wasn't in the mood to be manipulated by yet another powerful person. But what was the alternative? To walk out the door and continue to feel like a freak for the rest of his life? He took a deep breath and did as she asked.

"Now close your eyes and just relax."

Alex closed his eyes. A moment later he felt her hands gently position themselves under his head. He was surprised when he suddenly felt warm, peaceful feelings flow into his body. He saw colors whirling behind his lids, and the anxiety he'd been holding in his stomach unwound itself to the point where he felt so relaxed, it was as though he was melting into her table.

A few moments later, her fingers gently shook his shoulders. "I'm done, Alex."

He opened his eyes. "That's it?" he asked.

"Actually, you've been on the table for an hour."

His eyes widened in surprise. Before he could stop himself, he looked at his watch. Damn, he really had been on the table for an hour. He could have sworn he'd only been on it for five minutes.

"How do you feel?" Lena asked as she helped him sit up.

"I feel incredible. My heart doesn't hurt anymore, and I feel like—I don't know."

Lena laughed. "Your heart chakra was closed down. Someone must have recently broken it." When he looked at her in amazement, she chuckled. "Yes, Alex, I felt your broken heart. You took a chance and it didn't work. You're a very sensitive empath. You feel things deeper than most people."

"What exactly am I feeling? I'm so light and happy and calm."

"It's what everyone is looking for, Alex. It's love. But to those of us who understand, it's just energy. It's an experience of a higher vibrational energy."

He shook his head to himself. "That's amazing."

"Everything happens for a reason, Alex. It's no accident you chose Earthsong when you were looking for a solution to figure out why you are the way you are. As to what I did to you just now, it's really quite simple. I adjusted your energy using my energy. As an empath myself, I've learned that my energy is very strong, because I'm very sensitive to other people. I've learned my own sensitivities and the truth of what that means. I'm able to do these energy adjustments by being in a higher space in what many call light."

"Is that why I saw all that light when I had my eyes closed?"

"Yes."

He gave her a sheepish glance. "This may sound like a stupid question, but can you tell me why my heart hurt so much? Was it just because my heart chakra was closed down?"

"Because you wanted to be loved so badly, you took a chance to declare that to someone. You opened that door in your heart and declared, 'Here I am. Here's my light. Bring more light to me by sharing your own light.' But it didn't happen. Instead, the door was slammed shut. You took the energy of that and owned it."

He frowned. "I'm not sure I understand what you mean by owning it."

"You were hurt because this girl broke your heart. You felt like a victim of her rejection, correct?" He nodded. "That was your story. And you assigned that story to the hurt you were feeling. You gave it a job. Once you give energy a job, it attaches itself to your body. It turns chemical. The trick is to move the energy out of you before you give it a story, before it attaches and turns chemical."

"How do I do that?"

"You don't judge it. Judging attaches the story. Without that judgment, without that story, the energy doesn't have a job and swiftly moves through you. Now, you can move it once it attaches, but it's much harder."

"Wow. I really have a lot to learn." He paused. "Earlier you said these stones are your teachers. What exactly did you mean by that?"

"Everything is made of energy—the trees, the animals, the water we drink, the air we breathe, and even the earth we stand on. The problem is, we've forgotten this energy is all around us. And because we've forgotten that, we take this energy from each other through manipulation, drama, and neediness. When you held your stone, it grounded out the energy that was stuck in you because it reminded you of who you are. For many people, holding a stone is the first experience they have of actually feeling energy. Stones are wonderful teachers because a stone always knows what it is. A stone doesn't feel fear. People do. When you felt the fear leaving you, the crystal was teaching you that you no longer needed to feel fear."

"That may have been true in the beginning, but it certainly didn't help me this morning."

"In time, you'll learn that the stone is simply a reminder. The true place of power to move any emotion that isn't in your highest interest, including fear and victimhood, resides within you." She paused then continued, "There are many things we don't understand in this world. Some of these dark specters have been spoken of throughout history in myths, religions, and heroic sagas. At times they've been used to deliberately bring us to a place of fear, while others believe we actually created these dark shadows through our own fear. Nevertheless, as you had to learn, when your light and your energy were at their lowest, these dark creatures came knocking. Just like a predator stalking its prey. What did that teach you?"

He thought about it for a moment. "I learned I had to take a chance."

"And it brought you here. You had to trust your instincts."

"So what is this balancing thing you did to me?"

"I brought you to an energetic space that reminded you of how you're always supposed to feel. In this space you have no fear. You have no guilt, no anger. You are not a victim. Here, you felt the higher aspects of what you're capable of. You felt your courage, your strength, your curiosity, and your eagerness to learn. As I said earlier, at this moment, you're love in its purest form."

Alex marveled at the deep sense of peace and contentment running through his body. "Can you teach me this? Can I do this healing for myself and for others?"

"Of course you can. But first, let's focus on getting you to a better space."

"I already feel in a better space!" he exclaimed as he jumped off the table.

She chuckled. "Right now you do. But walk out that door, and with one wrong look or hurtful word from someone, and you'll find how quickly you can think yourself right back into a nasty, dark box." She walked him to the door. "There's one thing I want you to keep in mind at all times, Alex. It's what everything you've been through has been trying to teach you." She turned and looked at him. "You are always in control of your energetic experience. Your empathic ability will always tell you how you're doing."

Alex felt awesome all the way home. He couldn't believe how good he felt.

He turned on the radio. A song came on and he instantly felt his energy sink a little. It had been Angela's favorite song, and it evoked memories of her. He quickly turned the radio off, noting how quickly his energy had changed simply by remembering Angela.

Reaching the house, he put on the news and was met with a story about a fire that had killed a family, including three children and their pet. When they showed pictures of the little girls who had died, holding the dog that had also perished, Alex was so saddened that he felt his energy slip down a little further.

"Damn it," he shouted out. "I can't live my life this way."

Suddenly Lena's words drifted through his mind. *You are always in control of your energetic experience. Your empathic ability will always tell you how you're doing.*

It was true. He was allowing his judgment of the song and the news story to push him into that nasty, dark box.

Arriving at school the next day, his emotions felt raw. Walking down the corridor, he was acutely aware of everyone's energies. He could tell who was angry, and who was happy. In his first class, he had a knowing that his teacher wanted to be anywhere but where he was. What was happening? His energy was bouncing up and down according to what other people were feeling.

Suddenly it clicked, and Lena's words came back to him.

Glancing at the other students, he saw they weren't in control of their emotions. And he was feeling it. Why? Because, as Lena explained, he was a sensitive empath. He was physically feeling their projected thoughts, their emotions.

He knew he had a decision to make. He chose to be present to what he was feeling—he wasn't going to judge it or allow it to overwhelm him. He wasn't going to become a victim to it. He was going to stay in control of his judgments and the human habit of labeling all things either as good or bad, and simply witness what he was feeling.

To his shock, what he was feeling suddenly wasn't that bad. It was uncomfortable, but it wasn't overpowering him. He was taking charge of his experience by simply experiencing it. He realized that the less he judged the experience, the sooner it left his body. It didn't turn chemical, as Lena had explained to him. The lesson of the crystal was taking hold. Crystals don't fear. Crystals don't judge. They remind us of the vibration we are. Just as he felt on the mountain so many times before, the energy began to flow through him, leaving him calm and able to stay focused on what he was learning at that moment.

He was blown away by the simplicity of it all.

The week flew by and he found himself again at Lena's office.

"How are you doing?" she asked.

"I'm actually doing better. I had some experiences where I was starting to go into that dark place. I was physically feeling other people's thoughts and emotions. But I remembered what you said. I paid attention to what I was feeling, and didn't judge it. And when I didn't judge it, the uncomfortability flowed right through me."

"Excellent!" Lena exclaimed. "You're just gone through step one, which is realizing what you're experiencing. You're experiencing the darker thoughts and judgments of people as they try to control their own energetic situations from a place of their own wounds and pains."

"Why me?" he lamented.

She smiled. "It's obviously teaching you something. Nothing happens in a vacuum, you know." When she saw his face, she added, "I used to ask that very same question. But look at me now. I figured it out. I learned how it works; how I can be in total control of my energetic experience and make it a wonderful thing for me."

"How is that possible?"

"How do you feel when you come in here, Alex?"

"I feel wonderful. And curious. And eager to learn more."

"I rest my case. There are many parts to this. You need to go in steps. And I will help you along the way."

"I think I'm realizing something."

"What is that?"

He grinned at her. "I'm an empath, and I'll be okay."

On the way home, he deliberately put the radio on. When Angela's favorite song came on, he made himself listen to it. He was in control of this. He did feel a little sad, but it wasn't crippling. He allowed himself to experience what he was experiencing. And it wasn't that bad.

Yes, he still felt a little hurt that Angela had rejected him, but he wasn't giving the hurt permission to overwhelm him. He refused to give the hurt a job. Thanks to Lena, he realized he had options. He no longer needed to be a victim to what he was feeling.

This was better than protection salts or the smoky quartz. He laughed as he realized the power was inside him. It always had been. Yet, he'd needed to go through all he'd been through to reach that realization. To come to terms with his gift of empathy.

Alex came to the end of his stories. "Well, that's enough for one night. I hope it was helpful." The students agreed it was, and thanked him as they began to file out of the room. He turned to the girl and said, "If you want, stay after class, and we'll talk some more."

Once they were alone, he smiled at her. "You're an empath, my friend. You feel other people's emotions. You crave love. You have these strange sensations in your body—you feel like you're dying one minute, then the next you feel as though you could soar through the air. You feel so high and you feel so low. You're trying to figure out where you fit."

"How do you know all that?"

"Because I'm an empath, too."

"So what do I do about all of this?"

"I'm going to tell you the same thing that was told to me, which changed my life. Even if you don't know it yet, you are in control of your own energetic experiences. Your life has been designed to remember that simple truth."

"Does it ever get better?"

"You will learn to manage it. I will tell you, the darkness never fully lets go. There's a lot of darkness in this world, and it's not going away any time soon. To be honest, I've come to believe that because empaths know so much about energy—and we have no choice because we feel everything whether we want to or not—we were brought here to act as a counterbalance to the darkness. We can bring light into a dark space. I can look into your heart and see that light and compassion. We shine the light into the darkness. But we can do that only if we've learned to control our reactions to what we experience."

He closed his eyes for a moment and the woman gasped. "What's that feeling in my heart? What are you doing?"

He opened his eyes. "I'm opening my heart to you. I'm feeling your love and light. Instead of you feeling me freaking out, you're feeling me in an openness toward you. You're feeling my own love and light."

"Can I feel this all the time?"

"It takes practice. There are a lot of things out there that are going to make you not feel like this. There are things, or people, that don't want light shone on them. They prefer to operate in the shadows. They are the shadows. But you know what? In this space, right here, right now, there are no shadows. There's just you and me. And we're just being ourselves."

The woman sat back in her chair. "That is so cool. I guess I have a lot to learn. Hopefully you can teach me."

"I'll do my best."

She stuck her hand out. "My name is Zoey. When do I begin?"

He pointed to her heart. "You begin right there."

Afterword

There are so many complexities and challenges in life, yet none are more difficult to navigate than our emotions. Songs, poems, stories, actions, and experiences all lend themselves to the catalog of this emotional experience. Each is rooted in our sense cues of sight, touch, feel, taste, and hearing. The confusion begins when these trigger cues elicit an emotional experience that becomes overwhelming. Or worse, when these cues begin to dictate our every choice and our need to regain some kind of control of what is perceived as emotionally normal.

Examples of this include children who become overwhelmed because they aren't allowed to do what they want or are denied something they desire. Suddenly they're in a tantrum. Or the person who feels threatened when something or someone brings back a traumatic memory. They struggles to reclaim a sense of safety through the emotional fight-or-flight adrenaline rush.

Then there is the chemical release that creates a physical feel-good sensation whenever we fall in love. When it's not there, we crave it. This begins the emotional up-and- down experience, even driving some to numb their needs with substances if they can't attain that feel-good sensation.

Imagine all of this as the emotional soup of life, where all the ingredients compete, creating an unpleasant taste. Imagine those people who believe they are leading a bland, unexciting life, deliberately creating an emotional up and down in order to feel something or anything that they believe will add something to their existence. They create and live for drama.

What are these emotions? And how do our bodies experience them? In simple terms, science tells us that sense cues create an arousal of the nervous system. This in turn starts a process that releases the different chemicals of feeling according to what we judge our experience to be. Dopamine, serotonin, noradrenalin, acetylcholine, histamine, gamma-Aminobutyric acid (GABA), and glutamic acid are just some of the chemicals our human body releases. All of these take our body to a physiological response.

Love, anger, jealousy, envy, hate, lust, panic, shame, worry, embarrassment, courage, and anxiety all have their own chemical cocktail that adds to our physical experience. The heart begins to pound, breathing becomes shallow, and muscles tighten, and sometimes we escalate this process from anxiety to the point of panic. The opposite of this is what we call the desirable emotions, which contain their own chemical cocktail—the sensation of calm, bliss, happiness, true love. This is what we strive for. We all wish to live in an emotionally harmonious balance. But sometimes that desire seems so far out of our grasp.

It's not hard to see that this physical thing we call emotion is one of the driving forces of being human. Many things have been used throughout history to affect this process on the physical level. Alcohol, hallucinogenic plants, drugs, and medication all are designed to affect the chemistry of feeling. But what if, for some of us, this is just a stopgap or a diversion from the real experience that is unfolding? Is it possible there's another sense, an energetic sense in what science recognizes as the human auric field that adjusts energetically to its internally learned energy of experience? All of this is an attempt to control experience and keep itself safe. Maybe this auric field energetically extends and projects out, broadcasting like a radio in order to claim its space of safety and control. We've all seen cats when their hair stands on end. Could this be their radar sensing something? Their hair making them appear larger in order to attain safety and control over the environment?

Many empaths feel chills running up and down their spine for no apparent reason. How many times have you felt uncomfortable when someone or something seen or unseen has gotten too close—entering your personal comfort bubble? How often have you felt besieged by the energies from a crowd of people, from the news on TV, or from friends or family who live for drama? Those who deliberately create drama because that energy feeds them?

These are the energies that, as an empath, you feel on a daily basis. The choice each empath must make is how they will receive these energies. Will you judge what you feel, therefore, attaching to that energy and making it heavier? Or will you receive the energy without judgment? The empath who does not judge is more open energetically. This makes you more understanding of others' plights and needs.

In the bigger picture, negativity affects time and space. How do we know this? Because we feel so deeply the physical projection of this energy that it drives us to discover the opposite of this negative experience. We are driven to nature, to the arts, to seek solitude—whatever it takes to help us survive. We may not know it at the time, but we are learning something important in this energetic emotional boot camp.

One of the most important lessons is learning the difference between chemical experience and energetic experience. Imagine having the ability to affect your experience from a place of energetic choice rather than from the all-too-consuming emotionally chemical soup that the world lives its drama in. In other words, if you can catch the emotions you're feeling and simply witness them, without judgment, allowing them to flow swiftly through you, it doesn't allow the emotions to turn chemical in your body. Once anger, sadness, jealousy, or envy settles into your body, it's harder to get rid of.

Thoughts of darkness leading to more darkness, experiences of fear leading to more fear, and, worse yet, experiences of everything being so hopeless will surely trigger a chemical reaction in your body. Is there a choice? We say yes. In every moment lies the opportunity to choose how each moment is labeled or judged. That which is dark can be illuminated by a candle. That which is pain can be seen as trying to get your attention in order to elicit change. That which is fearful can be viewed as an opportunity to find your own courage.

There are so many reminders of this choice—stones, crystals, incense, darkness, light. But at the end of the day, the true reminder is you. The only wielder of light and truth is you. The barometer of life is you—the empath and your choices of life.

Life teaches you through trials and painful situations what your choices are. When you make negative choices, you are part of the same energetic problem as those who challenge you with their darkness and manipulation. But when you make choices from a higher state of energy and understanding, you become the candle that illuminates the darkness.

Remember—you always have control of your energetic experiences. Your empathic ability will always tell you how you're doing.

Thank you for taking this journey with us. You can reach us on our individual Facebook pages. You can also drop us a line at our website, www.comerfordwilson.com.

We love hearing from you!

Bety Comerford and Steve Wilson are ordained Spiritualist ministers, shamanic healers, psychics, teachers, and paranormal investigators with more than thirty years of experience helping people understand their empathic gifts. Many empaths feel a victim of their emotions and of those projected at them from others. They fear the darker aspects of their empathic journey. Bety and Steve help them understand that there is a better way to live their lives.